THE NEW THINKER'S LIBRARY

General Editor: RAYMOND WILLIAMS

POPULATION

POPULATION

BY

R. PRESSAT

LONDON
C. A. WATTS & CO. LTD.
1970

First published 1970

©
R. Pressat
1970

ISBN: 0 296 34837 6

Translated by Robert and Danielle Atkinson

Printed in Great Britain by
Alden & Mowbray Ltd
at the Alden Press, Oxford
36/635

PREFACE

Demography seems at first sight, to most people, an elaborate way of accounting for men and events (marriages, births and deaths), and a subject to which we more or less implicitly deny the status of a science. The layman wonders, no doubt, why the population, a body of individuals co-existing at a given time, should be the object of scientific consideration. After all, it must seem clear that it is at a much deeper level that the secret forces operate which make men reproduce, die and evolve in number and distribution on the planet.

Indeed, the first obstacle in understanding demography is the difficulty of conceiving the population as an object for scientific analysis and research. I have thought it useful, therefore, to introduce this work with the model writings of two precursors in the subject, Graunt and Malthus. These two, though from appreciably different viewpoints, both looked at certain problems of population in scientific terms.

Population is everywhere and nowhere in the sense that the biological, sociological, economic, historical and geographical aspects of demography could be studied simply as component parts of the disciplines concerned. But to bring together all the theories on population considered as a collection of individuals subject to process of evolution, has the advantage of throwing into relief the many interactions between the phenomena which activate a population and the varied characteristics of that population.

In the following pages I have tried to define some of these

links and interactions and I have chosen to pick out those aspects most likely to stimulate the interest of the reader who is comparatively new to the subject.

This type of treatment makes a certain amount of repetition unavoidable. My choice of chapter headings must also leave certain points somewhat obscure, but, in a work intended both as an introduction to the subject and as an invitation to critical thought, it was essential to avoid a dry catalogue of terms employed in a discipline which can, unless one is very careful, seem very dry indeed. It was necessary, rather, to arouse the interest of the educated reader in the important and varied implications of demography. To achieve this, certain guide-lines had to be laid down along which the theories thrown up by demography considered in its broadest sense could be put forward.

Furthermore, I think that true culture can only be based on precise information. Enough documentation, then, had to be assembled to support the various problems considered and to clarify the conclusions. Even more important, the reader had to be introduced to the language and the methods of measurement and analysis used by the demographer. This is why graphs and tables take up rather more space than would be desirable in a work devoted more entirely to philosophical speculation. A technical appendix has been included to cover those questions which could not be dealt with in the main body of the work without interrupting its general flow. Throughout the book, too, it will be found that narrative and descriptive passages alternate with more general considerations.

Perhaps it is as well to warn the reader that I have been mainly concerned with industrialized societies, not because I wish to minimize the importance of the present demographic problems of the Third World (which are mentioned and analysed from time to time), but because I want to give more general dimensions to this examination by considering more advanced societies. In any case, certain past situations which are studied historically are related in part to the situation of developing countries today.

R. Pressat

ACKNOWLEDGEMENTS

The translation of a technical text is always a difficult problem; fortunately Prof. Glass, who was good enough to encourage me to write this book, agreed to look over the English translation. He is responsible for a number of improvements for which I am most grateful. Any imperfections which remain are of course no fault of his.

R.P.

CONTENTS

I

GRAUNT AND MALTHUS

SOMEONE once observed that it is rarely possible to trace exactly the origin of a science. This does not, however, seem to be the case with demography, the beginning of which is very definitely marked by the publication in 1662 of John Graunt's *Natural and Political Observations Mentioned in a Following Index, and Made upon the Bills of Mortality, With Reference to the Government, Religion, Trade, Growth, Air, Diseases and the Several Changes of the Said City*.

There is no doubt, of course, that long before the middle of the seventeenth century both philosophers and politicians were showing concern about the size of a population, its desirable growth rate, and the means of influencing its evolution. Plato, for instance, recommended a static and precise demographic pattern for his ideal city. Confucius, in a China already a prey to overpopulation, favoured the idea of a quantitative equilibrium between the population and its environment. Moreover, the intervention of the state in this field is as old as the taking of censuses or the passing of laws to prevent population decline, as in ancient Rome with the Laws of Augustus.

However, until Graunt, population was more the object of vague thought and speculation than of observation and analysis. Without any self-knowledge, society developed, so it thought, under the influence of an unfathomable supernatural will. Graunt's positive researches were to go a long way towards changing this attitude and the fantasies which it induced. These researches were to be the starting point of the uninterrupted progress of that science of population which we call demography.

Graunt was not professionally engaged in scientific research. A prosperous and intelligent London cloth merchant, he interested himself in various social activities; he was, for instance, a major in the town militia. This relative independence from contemporary scientific circles and his personal commitment to civil life created especially favourable conditions for undertaking the type of research he was to make his own and which had never been even envisaged by his predecessors and contemporaries.

It was the *Bills of Mortality* which provided Graunt with the raw material for his researches. These weekly bulletins, the publication of which went back to the beginning of the sixteenth century, gave, every Tuesday, the lists of deaths (and sometimes births) recorded in the different parishes of London. From 1629 onwards, these lists gave some indication of the cause of death, as far as this could be established at the time by individuals lacking adequate knowledge. These tables reflected the current risks of mortality and were an extremely valuable indication in times of epidemic, especially the plague; they were used by the wealthy to indicate at what moment it would be wise to leave the towns for the healthier country. Graunt made these Bills of Mortality the object of scientific analysis on a surprising scale, considering that this type of study was completely new. The very explicit title of his work well shows the extent of the field covered by the author. Graunt was no mere statistical juggler and, in his hands, the tables of deaths became the means of determining the biological and socio-economic factors of mortality. Even more important, the recognition of statistical regularities in social and biological phenomena, and the complex of implications this holds for demography, started demographic statistics off immediately in one of its most important directions.

Among Graunt's statistical discoveries of permanent importance, his work on the ratio of the sexes at birth and among the
population as a whole is particularly noteworthy. Noting that
the number of men in a population was comparable to the
number of women (which was far from being evident in his
time), he established that the Christian religion was in accordance with the laws of nature in forbidding polygamy. Comparing births and deaths, he found that there were 13 of the
former for every 14 of the latter in London, but 63 births for
every 52 deaths in rural districts. Accordingly, it could be
established that the growth of the population in the capital
was due to the influx of people from the country.

The most remarkable result of Graunt's work, however,
was the drawing-up of the first life table. To achieve this,
Graunt had at his disposal some 230,000 cases of death which
had occurred between 1629 and 1638 and between 1647 and
1658 classified according to alleged cause of death, which was
sometimes far from being established scientifically. Graunt's
originality lies in the fact of his having used this classification
to establish an approximate distribution according to age, a
piece of deduction which is fairly simple with deaths caused
by illness in infancy but a much more delicate matter with less
specific causes. This is how he gives a rational account of the
course of death; according to him, out of every 100 births,
there survives:

at 6 years	: 64	at 56 years	: 6
16 ,,	: 40	66 ,,	: 3
26 ,,	: 25	76 ,,	: 1
36 ,,	: 16	80 ,,	: 0
46 ,,	: 10		

Graunt did not go as far as calculating the expectation of life
from this survival table. On the other hand, he did carry out
numerous demographic calculations which show his awareness

of the interdependence of population data. Identifying his life table with the classification of the population according to age, he attempted to estimate boldly the number of men capable of bearing arms. In addition, using the annual birth figures, he calculated the number of women of fertile age, then the number of families and finally the size of the population of London, which he estimated at 384,000 inhabitants. This was a very different result from the 6 to 7 millions suggested by some of his contemporaries.

If, on the whole, Graunt's conclusions are imprecise, the novelty and quality of his reasoning are clear. Moreover, the very fact of systematically studying a particular social reality was completely new. As we noted from the title of his book, this choice was wholly conscious: Graunt had no doubt about the utility of research such as his for achieving better government for men.

With this innovator in the subject, then, demography immediately assumes one of its principal roles, that of political arithmetic. Graunt's friend, Sir William Petty, was to develop this aspect by taking into consideration other collective phenomena of social life.

*

Today, Graunt's fame does not spread beyond the small circle of professional demographers. This is by no means the case with Malthus whose name, widely known, represents to the layman a certain type of concern about demographic evolution.

Malthus, an English parson born in 1766, is famous for his *Essay on the Principle of Population*, published anonymously in 1798 and which ran into five editions from 1803 to 1826. These later editions were much more documented and closely argued than the original, which had been essentially theoretical and more in the nature of a pamphlet.

Malthus's essay was written as a reply both to the *Enquiry Concerning Political Justice* of Godwin (1793) and to the *Esquisse d'un Tableau Historique des Progrès de l'Esprit Humain* of Condorcet. Both these works overflowed with optimism about the future evolution of reason, science, technical knowledge and the population, which, according to Godwin, would be able to find within itself regulatory techniques to avoid overpopulation.

To the idyllic scenes evoked by these two authors, the rather sombre picture of England at the end of the eighteenth century was a complete contrast. In the first place, the eighteenth century had been marked by a considerable growth in population. The estimates of Gregory King give the population as 5 million in 1700, while the first census in 1801 gives 9·2 million. This increase in population was the result of a fall in the mortality rate coupled with a rise in the birth rate which was due to an increase in the number of marriages stimulated perhaps by the favourable conditions created at the beginning of the industrial revolution. Some authorities consider that, with this growth of the population, there was a relative deterioration in the nutritional situation, for which the enclosure of the land was chiefly responsible. The enclosure of open fields meant the creation of pasture at the expense of land devoted to crops. The result of this was a declining calorific yield from the earth and increased production of meat, which was, in any case, inaccessible to the poorer classes. From being an exporter, England became an importer of corn. Secondly, prices rose more quickly than wages, and it became more difficult to import at the end of the century because the country was under blockade.

To complete the picture of the context of Malthus's essay, it is worth remembering the existence in England at that time of the system of public assistance known as the Poor Laws. These were long-standing laws which entitled the poor to public assistance and which after the Speenhamland meeting (1795) even became more generous. With the growth of public assistance the taxes imposed to pay for it increased from two million pounds in 1785 to four million in 1801.

It was this enormous difference between the glorious visions of Godwin and Condorcet and the sad reality of the England of the time which was to inspire Malthus to set forth his ideas in the edition of 1798 with ruthless sincerity – a sincerity which gained him permanent enemies and continues to do so. But let us trace the main thread of his argument.

Malthus began by pointing out the disparity between the possible growth of the population on the one hand and the means of subsistence on the other: the population may grow by geometrical progression, whereas the means of subsistence can grow only by arithmetical progression.

According to Malthus, the population grows geometrically by doubling every twenty-five years. This is put forward as a possibility and the author finds confirmation for his ideas in the case of the American population which enjoyed particularly favourable conditions for expansion. In contrast, food production at best can only increase arithmetically every twenty-five years by a constant amount equal to that produced initially. Malthus does not substantiate this at all, but it is not without some affinity to the famous law of diminishing returns.

This disparity between the two rates of growth in itself acts as a natural brake on unlimited demographic growth; Malthus wished to substitute a voluntary regulatory mechanism for this natural one. To be more precise, he wished to substitute 'preventive checks' for 'positive checks'.

These 'positive checks' are, in the first place, wars and exceptional occurrences which it is possible to avoid; but, in any case, the shortage of food constitutes the ultimate positive obstacle. Many of the 'preventive checks', however, have to be rejected, especially those termed vicious by Malthus, and which we know as adultery, prostitution, sexual deviation, birth control and abortion. The only 'preventive check' which Malthus approves of is what he calls 'moral restraint', prolonged celibacy coupled with chastity.

Up to this point, nothing in Malthus's analysis and the remedies he proposes could possibly give rise to scandal. The scandal was to come from certain apparently shocking assertions and particularly from this one:

A man who was born into a world already possessed, if he cannot get subsistence from his parents, on whom he has a first demand, and if the society do not want his labour, has no claim of *right* to the smallest portion of food, and, in fact, has no business to be where he is. At nature's mighty feast there is no vacant cover for him. She tells him to be gone, and will quickly execute her own orders, if he does not work upon the compassion of some of her guests.

The idea and the affirmation were to remain that the poor had no right to be sustained. This implacable principle formulated by Malthus and justified by the disparity in growth rates between population and subsistence, led the author to demand the abolition of the Poor Law, which he saw as an inefficient and damaging system, encouraging improvidence and generally worsening the situation. Since the time of Malthus there has been no lack of complaints by the rich on the improvidence of the poor . . .

Obviously, Malthus does not reject all individual aid, but thinks it should spring from private initiative and be used, preferably, for involuntary sufferers.

Malthus was to be even more criticized by his opponents for not favouring an egalitarian society, as Godwin had. The political principles he derived from his demo-economic analysis, in giving the owner classes an easy conscience, appeared to aim at strengthening the existing social order.

This interpretation of the theories of Malthus was to have enormous repercussions and has ensured that they have remained of interest to the present day.

*

Graunt and Malthus have taken us to the heart of the problems and practices of the science of population. It is not suggested that the whole range of demographic study can be opened up on the lines developed by these two innovators but the depth of their analysis will help us to grasp as a subject worthy of study that 'undiscoverable whole', population.

Graunt was predominantly interested in the statistical aspects of the subject. This element is, of course, absolutely essential, whether it be a question of counting individuals who constitute the whole or part of populations, or counting events which influence more or less directly the number and classification of these individuals: births, marriages, deaths and so on. Besides having their significance in the field of social knowledge, these statistical methods are related in a more or less complex way, which Graunt had noted and which must be analysed by the demographer.

However, man cannot be isolated from his environment either on the individual or on the collective level. It is to the credit of Malthus that he stressed the type of dependence which was for a long time the most pressing, that arising from the need for subsistence. At the same time, the matters under discussion assume much greater dimensions, so that the balance between population and subsistence appears bound up with the type of social organization.

More generally, the total understanding of what a population is and the workings of the phenomena which influence it, calls for investigation in a number of different directions. Almost every science can throw light on this field, while, in return, matters not specifically demographic can be clarified by the mechanics of demography.

These general considerations will be examined in greater detail in the course of the following chapters.

II

HOW THE WORLD IS POPULATED

IF we have little information about the precise way in which man evolved, the knowledge we have of the demographic evolution of humanity in its early stages is even more inexact.

Early civilization, dependent upon the simple gathering of food, hunting and fishing, could only support low population densities, varying from one inhabitant per 100 km² in the most difficult conditions (Eskimos) to one inhabitant per km² in the most favourable conditions, as in the coastal areas where the standard means of subsistence could be augmented with produce from the sea. It might usefully be added that in very early times climate was the main regulator of human evolution and its variations, which were quite considerable over a long period, can be found at the origin of the more important migrations.

In these conditions, at the dawn of the agricultural revolution, some 8,000 to 10,000 years B.C., the population of the world probably numbered somewhere between 5 and 10 millions.

The organization of land resources for agriculture, characterized by the practice of cultivation and the domestication of certain animal species, is a factor in demographic expansion, just as much as the urban revolution which first appeared in the Nile valley and in Mesopotamia about 4000 B.C. Estimates of world population at the beginning of the Christian era are very uncertain, varying most frequently between 150 and 300 million. The real situation, however, was probably nearer to the second figure than the first, if one can accept the

TABLE I. Estimated population of the world, by region (in millions)

Date	World Population	Africa	North America	Latin America	Asia (excluding USSR)	Europe (including USSR)	Oceania	Average annual growth rate
1650	553	60	1	10	380	100	2	} 3%
1750	726	68	1	15	500	140	2	} 6%
1850	1,325	88	26	35	900	274	2	} 5%
1900	1,663	110	81	63	980	423	6	} 5%
1950	2,509	207	167	162	1,384	576	13	} 8%
1960	3,010	257	200	212	1,684	640	17	} 18%

SOURCE: Goran Ohlin, *Historical Outline of World Population Growth*, Communication WPC/WP/486 of the World Congress on Population, Belgrade, 1965.

54 million inhabitants which Beloch attributes to the Roman Empire in the year 14, the 71 million which Durand gives for China in the year 2 and the 100 to 140 million considered by K. Davis as a plausible figure for India in the second century B.C.

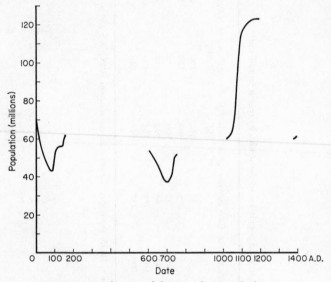

Fig. 1. Evolution of the population of China
(SOURCE: John Durand, The Population Statistics of China, A.D.2—1953)

The estimates for the beginning of modern times are much less variable. Taking the figure of 553 million which G. Ohlin gives for 1650 (see Table 1) it can be seen that there is only modest growth during the first seventeen centuries of the Christian era, the population only doubling itself over this period. The relatively precise observations which can be made at certain dates and in certain areas during this period throw some light on the hazardous course of the evolution of populations. In this respect, the data for China are particularly helpful (see Fig. 1). Covered very locally by censuses of uncertain standard, China appears to have undergone considerable fluctuations of population during the first fourteen centuries of the Christian era. The population of China was less in 1343 than it was in the year 2; in the meantime, however, it reached, according to the few statistics which have come down to us, figures varying from 1 to 3·5. It is possible that the destruction of certain smaller groups bears a relation to these fluctuations observed at national level in an important population group.

The real growth of the population of the world belongs, however, to modern times (see Table 1). Having approximately doubled between Christ's birth and 1650, it doubled again between 1650 and the beginning of the nineteenth century; and, more recently, it doubled in only sixty years, between 1900 and 1960.

The demographic history of the earth, then, after a confused beginning characterized by great fluctuations, appears in the long run to be the history of a more and more rapid growth, which has today taken on dramatic proportions. At the present rate of expansion (doubling every 40 years) the population of the world will reach the figure of 50,000,000,000 (about 400 people per square km!) which the most optimistic estimates give as the earth's population potential.

There is no doubt that the availability of means of subsistence must set an upper limit beyond which the population cannot grow in any permanent fashion, since famine would then become a regulating mechanism. (The state of autarchy in which human groups, sometimes very small ones, live, increases the number and severity of subsistence crises.) However, the manner in which the population has expanded cannot be entirely explained by the evolution of the means of subsistence. Two other factors come together to limit population growth: social disorders and epidemics. War, in its various forms, was the most usual cause of disturbance to the precarious social order which existed in the past. To remind ourselves of the different forms this could take, we have only to recall the invasions of Genghis Khan or of the Germanic tribes and, closer to us, the Thirty Years War.

But the greatest losses of human life were caused by epidemics. The most horrifying were those brought about by the plague, especially in its bubonic form. A great pandemic of this kind is known to have occurred towards the middle of the sixth century in the Mediterranean region. But it is the Black Death, which swept through Europe from 1347 to 1352 killing between a third and a half of the population, that has remained especially famous.

The distinction that has just been made between these three types of excess mortality must not blind us to the close connections existing between them. Thus, war was not only a killer because of the direct loss of human life it caused, but also because it left the invaded regions in a state of desolation. It is unlikely, too, that we shall ever be able to assess exactly the respective parts played by social disorganization and the introduction of epidemic diseases in the severe depopulation of Latin America which accompanied the European conquest.

Though fertility more or less compensates for losses through mortality, information about it always seems to have been much more concrete for the former than for the latter, giving it in some ways the status of a constant of the human species from the beginning of its history. The reconstructions of population behaviour which can now be undertaken, such as the comparison of populations not practising birth-control bring out important differences in biological aptitude and behaviour. Measured in terms of fertility – that is, the relation of the number of births to the number of women of child-bearing age – these differences take on a more precise significance. Briefly, in ancient western Europe, in France for example, the average offspring for a woman married at 20 was six children, while averages of eight or ten children seem to have been prevalent among other populations and at other times. If one remembers, too, that there may have been considerable variation in age at marriage and probability of marriage, it is easy to see that fertility has been (and still is in developing countries) as important a variable in the dynamic of populations as mortality.

In natural conditions, then, fertility and mortality virtually cancelled each other out. The slight demographic growth which could appear over long periods was partly or totally counteracted by periods of catastrophic excess mortality.

The developed countries of the West were to depart from this pattern of things in two distinct phases. First of all, the development of more adequate social and technical expertise (notably in the field of food production) caused the death rate to fall and, more especially, brought about a noticeable moderation in the concentrations of excess mortality. There is no doubt that such a phase can be observed in France and England during the eighteenth century

With the coming of the nineteenth century and especially during the latter half of it, we enter that important phase which has been called the demographic revolution, but which is more frequently termed today the demographic transition. Fig. 2 shows clearly that the death rate, which is initially slightly lower than the birth rate, fluctuates appreciably from one year to the next. It then begins to fall, but the birth rate only slows down later, and the difference between the two thus persists for several decades. We have to wait until the middle of the twentieth century to see the emergence of a new balance between the two similar to that existing at the beginning of the transition. However, the slight difference at present existing between the birth rate and the death rate is now smaller than during the two preceding centuries. This diagram (Fig. 2), valid for most countries in western Europe and the Anglo-Saxon countries overseas (in France, however, the birth-rate inexplicably started its decline some eighty years earlier) explains why the nineteenth century, and particularly its second half, was the period of greatest demographic growth.

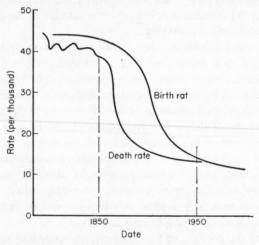

Fig. 2. The mechanism of the demographic transition

Taking the figures for the whole of Europe, the population grew from 180 million in 1800 to 400 million in 1900, despite considerable emigration, especially to America

The economically underdeveloped world, which comprises two-thirds of humanity, has not so far undergone this type of demographic revolution. Until recently the population situation in this sector of humanity was similar to the one previously known in industrialized countries. However, the changes in natural development which have been observed now for several decades are even more deserving of the description of revolution than those undergone by the European population in the last century. In the present case, however, the fall in mortality is not the result of increased control over environment but the result of intervention by more developed countries in the shape of medical aid. In other words, the declining death rate has not been the result of a slow advance in technical knowledge, but of the sudden intrusion of effective techniques developed elsewhere. This upsetting of the traditional demographic balance has had certain disturbing effects. Since the birth rate has remained unchanged, the growth of the population has reached prodigious proportions; a doubling of the population every twenty-five years has become common (during the last century in Europe, no population doubled in less than fifty years).

Finally, the 3,500,000,000 people alive now present us with a picture of a world in constant motion, on the social and technical planes, as well as the demographic. Some 55,000,000 people are added every year to this impressive total, and the distribution of this population changes continually, moving further and further away from a distribution related to the resources provided by the natural environment: questions of climate, fertility of the soil or the availability of energy and water no longer play the same part as before in determining the location of populations. The concentrations of population demanded by the highly-organized nature of working conditions in modern times and the requirements of a much more extensive social life, are now much more feasible because of the greatly increased volume of transport available; but, at the same time, they tend to alienate man from nature. But this movement, in its turn, makes demographic problems so much more interesting.

III

DEMOGRAPHIC STRUCTURES AND SOCIAL STRUCTURES

AGE is one of the fundamental demographic variables. A determining factor in the process of human reproduction and the increasing proportion of old people in the world, it plays an essential part in the analysis of the dynamics of a population.

Further, it is not only the vital capacities which are linked to age: all important mental and biological functions evolve with it, which explains the vast number of analyses which refer to it.

Society has always attached great importance to the age of individuals, but there has been a great change in the system of values built around this subject, especially since the considerable fall in the death rate. In a population where attaining and passing the age of sixty, let alone eighty, could be looked on as something of an exploit, a kind of veneration surrounded the man who could thus escape the terrible obstacles which life had placed in his way: the oldest could only be the strongest, the wisest and in every way a sort of superman, an exceptional repository of human knowledge and accumulated experience.

Today, what used to be phenomenal has become commonplace. The new-born in the eighteenth century had only twenty chances in a hundred of living beyond the age of sixty and only three in a hundred of reaching eighty, while soon respectively 90 per cent and 45 per cent of persons born will live beyond these ages, which as a result are no longer invested with the same glamour. In the past, because of the omnipresence of death, an individual could never enjoy the

18

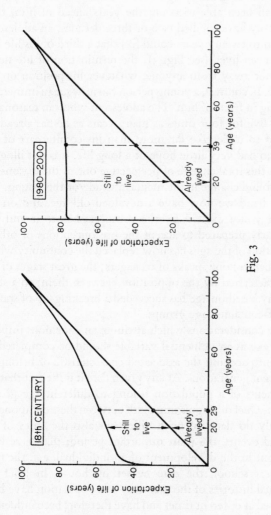

Fig. 3

feeling of a long life lying in front of him. If a newly-born being had been able to count the years ahead of him, they would only have totalled two or three decades; an adolescent of fifteen to twenty years could feel that a third of his life had already been lived (see Fig. 3); the termination of life never seemed far away from anyone, whatever his position on the age scale. In contrast, a young person can now see an immensity stretching in front of him. The adolescent who can reasonably hope to live for four times as many years as he has already is prepared to undertake far more than his counterpart of the past, who had very little hope of a long life. It is not illogical to see in this total change of perspective one of the reasons for the profound change in the mental attitude of the young. On the one hand we now have a devalued old age, and on the other, a youth excited by the prospects before it and not particularly prepared to accept the preconceptions of others. Segregation of the ages has now replaced the continuity which existed before: one speaks of teenagers; the great stages of life are characterized by the opposition between them; to a strict hierarchy based on age has succeeded a breaking-up of society into self-contained age groups.

These considerations which attribute an enormous import-ance to age as an influential variable should be completed by taking into account the associated characteristic of belonging to different generations. At any given date it is the fact that the components of a population belong to different age groups that is the chief distinguishing mark between these components. Not only do dates of birth differ but also the dates of the principal events, the most important periods that have been significant in the development of an individual, e.g. the time he was at school, the date he set up house. In brief the individual histories of the members of a population have been composed at different times and have therefore been influenced differently, especially during periods of important cultural and social change. The so-called conflict of the generations, those differences in their response to the outside world, has, finally, a dual origin: the variable position of individuals on the age-scale, influenced, as they are, by past experience and their different hopes for the future; and secondly, the fact that integration into the social order has taken place at different periods and in different environments.

To be at all pertinent, any analysis of social patterns should refer to these essentially demographic concepts, which in turn should benefit our understanding of the mechanism of demographic evolution. It is in this way that demographers can learn to distinguish between phenomena which are fixed in time and those which are subject to change, and can thus avoid the temptation of granting an exclusive role to age. We must now look at a specific example of these general considerations.

The Population Pyramid

The distribution of a population at a given time by the age and sex of its components is one of its most important characteristics and has many social and economic implications.

This method of dividing the population is usually represented graphically by a population pyramid, the abscissa indicating the numbers of people and the ordinate the ages; to each age-group of each sex, therefore, there corresponds a rectangle which is as long as the numbers of the group are large.

The general shape of the pyramid is a triangle. This is simply because of the mortality factor which progressively reduces the numbers of the generations as they get older, or, in other words, as they move towards the upper reaches of the pyramid. But many other factors do intervene which explain the more or less irregular shape of these pyramids and it can be said that the shape of a pyramid embodies the essentials of the last eighty years of the history of the population it represents.

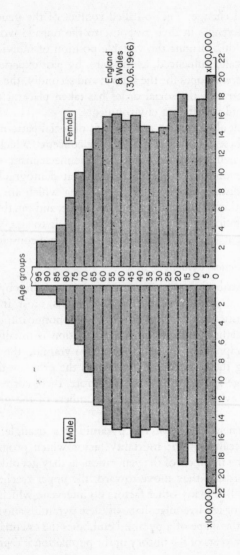

Age groups

Female

England
& Wales
(30.6.1966)

Male

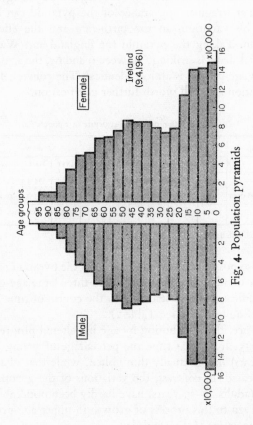

Fig. 4. Population pyramids

Fig. 4 consists of population pyramids for England and Wales on 30 June 1966 and of Ireland on 9 April 1961. The classically triangular shape has been perceptively modified; in particular, certain older elements are larger than younger ones. This rather irregular appearance of the pyramid can be explained by variations in the birth-rate and the effects of migration. Taking the pyramid for England and Wales, its cylindrical shape is striking; between 0 and 65, the size of the different age-groups is almost identical. The consequences of this situation are well worth further clarification.

TABLE 2. Evolution of the age-structure of a population

Age group	England and Wales				France				
	1695*	1821*	1841	1966	1775*	1851	1901	1946	1966
0–19 years	47·8	49·0	46·1	30·7	42·8	38·5	34·3	29·5	33·5
20–59 years	41·5	43·5	46·7	51·3	49·9	51·3	52·7	54·5	48·8
60 years and over	10·7	7·5	7·2	18·0	7·3	10·2	13·0	16·0	17·7
All ages	100·0	100·0	100·0	100·0	100·0	100·0	100·0	100·0	100·0

* Approximate figures

It is also possible to present the data in the pyramid numerically; by dividing the population into three large age-groups, the modification of its structure in the course of time can be followed quite easily (see Table 2).

In France, the distribution by age has altered progressively since 1775; from that time the percentage of young people (0–19 years) has gradually diminished, while that of the old has increased. In contrast, the variations of the group in the middle (adults 20–59 years) have hardly been noticeable. The name given to this process of growth in upper age-groups is called the *ageing of the population*.

It may be seen that the ageing process started about two centuries ago in France, while in England nothing very marked appeared before 1841.

Why do these differences occur and, more generally, what causes this ageing of the population?

The first and most natural idea is to attribute this process to the lengthening of human life; but this does not explain why such changes have not been similar in two neighbouring countries with a similar record of progress in the fight against mortality. Closer analysis, however, shows that the drop in the death rate has only had a slight influence on changes in the structure of the population, because such a fall means a gain in human lives at all ages (this being particularly noticeable in the lowest age groups, infant mortality dropping very appreciably, in extreme cases, from 200 to 250 per 1,000 to 20 or even 15). In fact, it is the fall in fertility which initiates the ageing process: the proportion of the old in the population grows in relation to the rest because the number of young children gradually diminishes. This mechanism is sometimes expressed more vividly by saying there is ageing at the base (of the pyramid, that is). In future, when illnesses caused by degeneration (cardio-vascular trouble for example) can be checked in their development, there will be a fall in mortality among advanced age-groups. This will entail ageing at the summit (of the pyramid).

An even more complex situation can be observed in France: ageing, measured by the growing size of the 60 year and over age-group, can occur at the same time as rejuvenation, which expresses itself in a growing percentage of under-twenties. This happened in France between 1946 and 1966 and was a result of a rise in the birth rate which started in the first of those two years.

Migration can also be a factor in the modification of the age-structure of populations. Emigration is usually a cause of ageing and immigration usually brings rejuvenation. When differences in fertility exist in populations between which there is migration, very marked differential ageing can result.

These two factors, however, often act in opposite directions and the final effect may be negligible. But let us look now at the examples where differential ageing occurs between different categories of the same population (see Table 3).

In this example, the higher fertility of the country has not been able to counteract completely the effect of ageing caused by the intense emigration to which it is subject. In Sweden,

TABLE 3. Percentages of persons aged 65 and over.

Sweden			France (1946)	
Years	Country	Town	Rural districts	12·8
1900	9·0	6·0	towns with less than 5,000 inhabitants	10·7
1930	9·9	7·7	towns with 5,000 to 10,000 inhabitants	9·8
1945	11·0	8·4	towns with 10,000 to 50,000 inhabitants	9·4
			towns with more than 50,000 inhabitants	8·6

SOURCE: *The ageing of populations and its economic and social consequences*, United Nations, 1956.

during the last 45 years, the difference between town and country has remained more or less constant; in France, by 1946, the degree of ageing rises as the number of inhabitants falls.

The population of Ireland, taken at two very different dates (1841 and 1961), is a perfect example of a population whose age structure has been completely upset by a fall in fertility coming at the same time as a heavy emigration such as that following the severe famine of 1846–48 (see Fig. 5).

The concept of ageing of a population has a wide relevance as does the concept of population itself. In other words it can

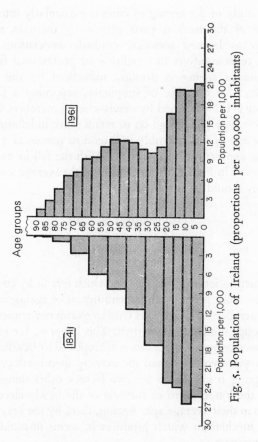

Fig. 5. Population of Ireland (proportions per 100,000 inhabitants)

be applied to more restricted groups than national population such as the working population, the electoral population and so on.

The study of the ageing of élites is particularly interesting because of the leading parts played by them in society, whether as learned societies, graduate associations or as elected representatives in a political or professional field. In this instance ageing is strongly influenced by the fall in mortality: for the sake of simplicity, supposing a political assembly is being formed by newly-elected members with an average age of 35 who go on to retain office indefinitely, the average age of this assembly will tend to remain at 35 years plus the expectation of life at 35. With the fall in mortality as observed in France, the evolution of the average age in this assembly would be as follows:

> 18th century: 60 years
> mid-19th „ : 66   „
> 1960   : 74   „.

Learned societies and academies which recruit by co-option are even more prone to the phenomenon of ageing in so far as the members of such bodies tend to recruit newcomers from age groups similar to their own. This happens, for instance, if deceased or outgoing members are replaced by new members twenty years younger than the existing membership. In this case ageing is influenced by two factors, other things being equal: the longer term of survival of the newly-elected and the rise in their average age. Ageing, then, by the very nature of the mechanism which produces it, seems unavoidable in most instances.

This is particularly true at the level of national populations. To begin with, the fall in the birth-rate is an absolute necessity in order to contain humanity within the vaguely conceived limits imposed by the finite dimensions of the earth. This means inevitably that the process of ageing must become more and more marked. The dilemma can be expressed thus: to increase or to age? The choice of the latter is inevitable. And secondly, in the future the fall in mortality will (contrary to the effect of the fall during the past two centuries) become another factor in the ageing process.

In this regard, the population projections prepared by the Royal Commission on Population in 1947 are extremely illuminating. Falling mortality combined with the maintenance of fertility at the low level current at that date would cause the percentage of individuals over 65 to increase in one century from 10·4 per cent to 21·5 per cent! Simple calculations show that if the population of western countries became stationary at a level corresponding to a life-expectancy of eighty years, its composition by age would be as follows:

0–19 years	25 per cent
20–59 ,,	50 ,, ,,
60 years and over	25 ,, ,,
All ages	100

It is obviously possible to envisage an even greater imbalance in favour of the aged, if we imagine what the death-rate of the human species might be in fifty or a hundred years or more. However, such speculation is unhelpful unless it takes account of possible improvements in the quality of life at advanced or even very advanced ages. If a perceptible prolongation of human life is accompanied by a corresponding improvement in the health of the aged, then these added years of life will have quite different economic and social consequences from those envisaged at present arising from the preservation of a higher proportion of old people in precarious circumstances.

The Consequences of Ageing

We have now reached the point where we must examine the various consequences of the process of ageing of populations and its inevitable progress in the future.

This kind of analysis takes us back, first of all, to the differentiation of individuals by age and generation of birth. The greater the relative importance of aged persons in a population, the more important will be the influence of their ideas, their attitudes and their behaviour. Less willing to change, because of habits already well-established, the type of education received and the limited horizons in front of them, the older generations generally form the conservative elements of societies. The most obvious manifestations of this phenomenon occur during elections and the introduction of the vote for women has only intensified them. In addition to the fact that the female population is more attached to tradition than the male, its demographic weight at the older ages is also greater because of greater longevity. In other words, the electoral body has been aged by the enfranchisement of women.

The consequences of ageing are even greater when it is related to select social groups occupying key positions in society. Earlier, we looked at the ageing of learned societies which, if they are to play a leading part in the intellectual life of a country, should ideally bring together men who are well-informed about the latest developments in the disciplines they represent, which is generally not the case with older people whose education took place in the past and whose capacity for adaptation is diminished. Some societies have very wisely fixed an upper age limit at which members are obliged to leave the society.

This tendency towards the pre-eminence of older people in leading positions eventually leads to gerontocracy; the term is usually employed pejoratively, a fact which has its origin in the disadvantages of concentrating leading and influential positions in the hands of older people. This has not always been the case, as we have seen; at one time considerable prestige was attached to old people, who were justly considered to be repositories of experience, knowledge and wisdom which could only be transmitted orally and directly. Thus in societies in which the elders were considered the best guides the evolution and renewal of thought and techniques were so slow as to be almost imperceptible. In this context, the dominant characteristic of such societies was the transmission of permanent truths which were certainly better understood and more deeply felt by those who had had more time to assimilate them.

Up to this point, we have been chiefly concerned with the psychological consequences of the process of ageing, and this has shown up a certain paradox. The ageing process, a characteristic of modern developed countries, is an obstacle to development in so far as it values old ways and is opposed to the changes which are an absolute condition of progress. In traditional societies, on the other hand, where power was usually and very justly confided to the elders, this process would have accentuated the pre-eminence of the oldest portion of the population, but, in fact, this could not occur because of the constant level at which fertility was maintained.

Another characteristic of ageing populations is their slow rate of renewal. We have said that an ageing population is characterized by a declining birth-rate; now, a population whose birth-rate is, say, 40 per 1,000, renews 40 per thousand or 4 per cent of its components every year, whereas a Malthusian population with a birth rate of 15 to 20 per thousand only renews 1·5 to 2 per cent of its elements. A population changes and develops as fast as the relative weight of the new elements is great. Here again the ageing population is at a disadvantage, not because of the fact of ageing itself, but because of the direct effect produced by ageing – the fall in fertility. But however important the age-distribution of a population may be as a determining factor in the collective psychology of that population, it is usually the economic and social factors in the grouping which attract most attention.

Individual consumption and production varies distinctly with age. Consequently, national production and consumption are appreciably affected by the age-structure of a population. Young and old usually consume less than adults, but their production is almost negligible. From the relationship

$$\frac{\text{Adults}}{\text{Total population}}$$

we can gain a rough idea of the way in which the age-structure of a population may influence the standard of living. In fact this relationship varies very little; according to the data in Table 2, in England and Wales during the last 250 years, it has only varied between 41·5 and 51·3 per cent, and in France, between 48·8 and 52·7 per cent. To go any further than this, the exact nature of the activities of the population would have to be determined, that is, the exact proportion of people, at every age, exercising an economic function. If we established the activity rates in this way, we should find that they vary with the economic development of the country, which is, in turn, related to the rate of population growth. The highest population growth-rates are found in developing countries where the population is youngest; economic activity starts earlier than in industrialized countries and under-employment occurs in all age groups. Studies taking these factors into account show that the active proportion of the population can vary from 40 to 78 per cent of the total population.

The problem of responsibility for the young and aged does not arise in the same way in developed countries, which we shall be looking at in greater detail. In these countries, where the family unit has lost some of its earlier functions, responsibility for the aged is most frequently assumed by society as a whole by means of a redistribution of income, a typical example of which is the retirement pension. The system of retirement pension based on contributions to a superannuation fund can give the impression that each individual builds up his own pension and that when the time for retirement comes asks nothing of anyone. In fact, since his retirement pension is

TABLE 4. Equivalent ages of retirement in 1940

	France: 60 years	France: 65 years
England and Wales	58 years	63 years
Germany	57 ,,	62 ,,
Switzerland	57 ,,	62 ,,
Italy	56 ,,	62 ,,
Holland	56 ,,	61 ,,
Canada	55 ,,	60 ,,
United States	55 ,,	60 ,,
U.S.S.R.	51 ,,	56 ,,

only made possible by transference from the current annual product, it is indeed a question of redistribution. And the spread of this type of retirement pension, necessitated by the constant devaluation of money, makes this aspect much more real. Taking the amount of the retirement pension to be 50 per cent of the gross salary during the years of activity, the amount to be paid into the superannuation fund varies from 1·5 to 10 per cent, according to the prevailing demographic condition.

Another way of stressing the inequality of populations with regard to the problem of retirement is to calculate, following P. Vincent, the equivalent ages of retirement on the basis of

equal contributions to the retirement fund. Table 4 presents
the situation in 1940.

If it were possible to go into the details of specific needs at
every age, it would be easier to judge the extent of the
influence of the particular age-structure of a population, and
especially the way in which ageing induces a declaration of
vital activity. One sector where consumption and needs are
most influenced by the process of ageing is that of medical
care. More and more efficient and expensive methods of
preserving life, such as the increasingly frequent and necessary
hospitalization of older patients, make it a vain hope that we
shall ever be able to give to everyone the best care made
possible by medical science. Although all societies are still
very far from providing adequate health and social protection
for their old people, the costs of this service, together with
those of educating the young, constitute one of the longest
items of public expenditure.

It is possible, of course, to distinguish many other types of
demographic structure besides that of age. There are those
of sex, marital status, duration of marriage and so on. Furthermore, knowledge of the distribution of population according
to combined demographic characteristics is extremely valuable, and age is often a variable in this context.

These general considerations can be illustrated by one particularly vivid example. In studying the distribution of population by sex and age (as with the population pyramid in its
classic form) certain disparities in numbers between sexes may
appear in certain age-groups. Such disparities, when they
occur at ages at which marriage generally takes place, can
obviously lead to the appearance of a larger number of single
persons than usual among the sex with the greatest numbers,
since it has obviously been impossible for everyone to arrange
a marriage with a member of the opposite sex. This sort of
situation can easily occur in a country subject to immigration.

Where immigration is not of whole families, men tend to predominate among the immigrants; and therefore come to constitute a majority sex; consequently not all of them can marry. In contrast, the minority of women are advantageously placed for marriage and do in fact achieve it more frequently than men. The same mechanism acts in the opposite direction in countries subject to emigration.

The following data on the frequency of single persons in the 45–49 years age group in a number of countries affected by migration at a time when the generations in question were of marriageable age, confirm the statements made above. The first three countries are emigration countries and the last one (Canada) is an immigration country.

Percentages of single persons in the 45–49 years age-group
in 1950

	Males	Females		Males	Females
Norway	15·5%	20·4%	England and Wales	9·8%	15·2%
Italy	9·3%	15·0%	Canada	13·2%	11·7%

These are examples of a situation in which a demographic phenomenon (nuptiality) and the population structure it brings about (division of the population by marital status) are considerably influenced by the existence of another type of demographic structure (division by sex and age). It would be possible to give examples of the influence of ageing on social structures in the broadest sense: division of the population by level of education, occupation, place of residence, religious denomination, and so on. All these would seem to be largely determined by the phenomenon of the renewal of generations and are thus linked to the age-structure of the population which results from the process of renewal.

It seems absolutely necessary, then, to take demographic

structures, especially age structure, into account in all analysis of social patterns. Clarifying the relations between the demographic aspects of a population and the many factors which influence it cannot but lead to a deeper and more complete understanding of society.

IV

INEQUALITY IN THE FACE OF DEATH

INEQUALITY in the face of death: with this striking expression the Swiss demographer Hersch stigmatized the worst form of injustice suffered by the human race. However, the existence of this inequality, as well as the realization that it does exist, seem to be of comparatively recent date. Such eminent thinkers as the naturalist Buffon, himself the compiler of a life table, took it as a given fact that the mighty, the humble, the rich and the poor were all equal in death.

It is certainly true that, until recent times, social inequality did not too seriously aggravate the risks of mortality among the lower classes. Because of the ineffectiveness of medical care, the poor lost very little by not being able to take advantage of it. The great epidemics spared no one and the standard of hygiene at the court of Versailles was probably no higher than in country districts. The crisis of subsistence was probably the only plague which did not affect the rich, whose dietary habits could be disastrous anyway.

When we come to present times, however, differences in mortality should not be attributed exclusively to social factors. On the one hand, numerous variables, linked to environment and behaviour (climate, population density, diet) intervene, though the exact part played by these different factors can never be known. And secondly, genetic factors also create inequality in death, at least at the individual level.

The data gathered by Dublin, Lotka and Spiegelman in *Length of Life* (p.42) yield the following table for the evolution of average expectation of life through the ages.

This table is not entirely reliable, especially in respect of the very early periods: the statistics are too fragmentary to represent an epoch or even a civilization; and in any case the fluctuations in the death-rate were too considerable to be summed up in one figure.

Nevertheless, it is the case that the average length of life

Period	Area	Author	Average life
Early Iron and Bronze Age	Greece	Angel	18 years
About 2,000 years ago	Rome	Pearson	22 years
Middle Ages	England	Russell	33 years
1687–91	Breslau	Hally	33·5 years
Before 1789	Massachusetts and New Hampshire	Wigglesworth	35·5 years
1838–1854	England and Wales	Farr	40·9 years
1900–1902	United States	Glover	49·2 years
1946	United States	Greville	66·7 years
To which we can add one of the latest and best results recorded:			
1961–1965	Sweden		73·6 years

never remained permanently under 20 years, which would have entailed the disappearance of the human species, and that at present it stands at between 70 and 75 years in most developed countries. This appreciable lengthening of the expectation of life at birth is the most tangible result of the progress of western civilization.

Social Mortality in the Past

The lack of knowledge of the exact death-rate at very early periods is accompanied by a total ignorance of the differences in death rate which may have existed between particular sections of the population. It is for the upper classes that it is

TABLE 5. Expectation of life at birth

British nobility			England and Wales		
Cohort born	Male	Female	Cohort born	Male	Female
1550–1574	36·5	38·2			
1575–1599	35·3	38·1			
1600–1624	32·9	35·3			
1625–1649	31·2	33·2			
1650–1674	29·6	32·7			
1675–1699	32·9	34·2			
1700–1724	34·4	36·2			
1725–1749	38·6	36·7			
1750–1774	44·5	45·7			
1775–1799	46·8	49·0			
1800–1824	49·2	51·7			
1825–1849	52·1	58·4	1840–1	39·9	43·1
1850–1874	54·7	62·8	1860–1	42·3	46·2
1875–1899*	53·8	67·0	1875–6	46·1	50·9
			1890–1	48·8§	54·5
1900–1924†	60·2	70·0	1910–1	55·2‖	61·0
1925–1949‡	61·9	71·0			

* Mortality after age 80 assumed the same as in the previous cohort
†   „   „   „   53   „   „ „ „ „ „   „   „
‡   „   „   „   30   „   „ „ „ „ „   „   „
§ Mortality after age 70 assumed the same as in the epoch 1956–60
‖   „   „   „   50   „   „ „ „ „ „   „   „

first possible to establish reliable statistical information; this is due to the existence of records for these privileged groups in which births, marriages and deaths were recorded. Hollings-worth's careful study of the British nobility came to the conclusions given in Table 5. A comparison with the popula-tion of England and Wales as a whole is only possible from 1840, when the difference is 13 years for men and 15 years for women in favour of the aristocracy. The difference is thus quite considerable and there is no reason to believe that it had not been so for a long time, though perhaps less marked. It is doubtful whether expectation of life went beyond 25 for the population as a whole during the sixteenth and seventeenth centuries, while it went well beyond 30 and even reached 35 during the eighteenth century (averages for the population as a whole have been arrived at by taking the arithmetic mean of the figures given for men and women). It is possible to see among the aristocracy the persistence of a longer average life for women than for men (except for 1725–49). This is a fact which has always been noted in almost all groups where mortality rates have been measured. The difference is parti-cularly marked in periods where the aristocracy has been more than usually affected by military losses.

Other studies of the ruling classes have stressed their privileged situation as far as the death-rate is concerned; thus, among the bourgeoisie of Geneva, the situation seems to have been even more favourable than among the British aristo-cracy.

First noticeable among the upper classes, the phenomenon of social differences in mortality was only really seen by contemporaries during periods of great upheaval as, for instance, the wars at the end of the reign of Louis XIV, as Vauban testifies in his *De l'influence de la misère sur la mortalité*, and particularly during the industrial revolution in western Europe. In this latter instance, fast-growing and anarchic urbanization, deplorable conditions in factories, low wages, insecurity and child labour were all factors in producing conditions of such wretchedness that even the least concerned elements of society could hardly fail to be conscious of the inequality in the risks of death.

A vast amount of literature of dubious scientific value was devoted to the subject: in France, for instance, *La mortalité dans les classes indigentes* (1828) and *Le tableau de l'état physique et moral des ouvriers* (1840) by Villermé. It was only much later

TABLE 6. Mortality in Paris, by district

Districts	Standardized mortality rates per 1,000 inhabitants*		Percentage fall
	1817	1850	
well-to-do (1,2,3,4)	24·9	18·2	27
intermediate (5,6,7,10,11)	27·3	25·1	8
poor (8,9,12)	36·5	33·7	8

* Standardized to take account of differences in the age-structures of the population.
SOURCE: E. Vedrenne-Villeneuve, 'L'inégalité sociale devant la mort dans la 1ère moitié du 19ème siècle', *Population*, 1961–4.

that the question was taken up again in a quantitatively satisfactory manner. Thus, it has been possible to demonstrate that the fall in the death-rate in Paris during the first half of the nineteenth century was much more considerable in well-to-do areas than in the poorer districts (see Table 6), which had been 47 per cent higher in 1817, 85 per cent higher in 1850 than in the wealthy districts.

Finally, it has been shown that class-specific mortality reached its peak during the nineteenth century at a time when the privileged classes were beginning to benefit from the progress of hygiene and medicine and an increasingly high standard of living, while at the same time a miserable urban proletariat was being created. At the present time, however, it seems that the differences in the risks of death are even smaller than before the industrial revolution. Still referring to Paris and using the findings of Hersch and Sauvy, it can be seen that the death-rate, 47 per cent higher in the poor districts than in the rich around 1820, went up to 85 per cent around 1850 and dropped to 42 per cent around 1890 and finally to 26 per cent around 1946.

The Present Situation

The perceptible diminution of social class differences in mortality, noticeable between the middle of the last century and recent years, seems almost certain to continue, but with slight variations.

In England and Wales, where research on social factors in mortality has been more extensive than anywhere else since the initial stimulus given by Dr. W. Farr in 1839, one can follow the development of differential mortality very closely. For official surveys, the Registrar General traditionally divides the population into five classes which can be summed up thus:

I   Professional, etc., occupations
II Intermediate occupations
III Skilled occupations
IV Partly skilled occupations
V   Unskilled occupations

Married women are classified according to the occupation of their husbands.

Table 7 shows how the range of mortality changed between 1921–23 and 1950 for men and married women aged between 20 and 64.

There is very little variation for men between 1921–23 and

1950: ranging from 82 to 125 at the first date, the difference only varies from 86 to 118 at the second. However, if a comparison is made between 1930–32 and 1950, the picture is very different for both men and women. The mortality scale does not correspond to the social hierarchy. While mortality

TABLE 7: Comparative mortality of men and married women of 20–64 years in England and Wales

| | | Social categories | | | | | |
		I	II	III	IV	V	Total
Men	1921–23	82	94	95	101	125	100
	1930–32	90	94	97	102	111	100
	1950	98	86	101	94	118	100
Married women	1930–32	81	89	99	103	113	100
	1950	96	88	101	104	110	100

SOURCE: *The Registrar General's Decennial Supplement, England and Wales, 1951: Occupational Mortality*, Part II, vol. 1, Commentary, London, 1958.

rose regularly from class I to class V in 1921–23 (and again in 1930–32 among married women), the situation has changed completely in 1950 where class II is in the most favourable position and class IV overtakes classes I and III as far as men are concerned.

When one looks at the death-rate in old age (65 and over), the disparity between social hierarchy and mortality scale is even more striking. The following are the results for 1950:

	I	II	III	IV	V	Total
Men Married	109	97	104	99	93	100
women	101	95	100	110	95	100

In this example, class V is in the most favourable position. Social inequality in death, though still apparent at an early age, disappears in old age. It will be seen, however, that this conclusion is not universally valid.

Examining the causes of death more closely for adults (20 to 64), certain causes appear with proportionately greater frequency the lower one goes down the social scale. This is the case with pulmonary tuberculosis, syphilis, cancer, stomach ulcers, pneumonia and bronchitis. In contrast, cancer of the prostate, kidney and bladder, heart diseases caused by arteriosclerosis, high blood pressure and diabetes become more frequent as one ascends the social scale.

It appears, then, that the symptoms of ageing and bodily wear are more prevalent in the upper reaches of the social scale, where, on the other hand, there is better protection against easily avoidable illnesses such as infectious diseases.

Are we to take it, then, that the people with the heaviest responsibilities in society, and who for this reason belong to the upper classes and enjoy considerable material benefits, are more likely to age prematurely under the weight of their duties? This interpretation is not confirmed by an interesting study by the Metropolitan Life Insurance Company.[1] The statisticians of that company have compared the death-rate among eminent men in *Who's Who in America* with the death-rate in the various occupational categories to which these men belong. Thus, the mortality of the business executives appearing in *Who's Who* is only 48 per cent of that of the profession as a whole, that of educationalists 80 per cent, judges and lawyers 71 per cent, men of letters 78 per cent, physicians and surgeons 65 per cent, engineers 37 per cent and scientists only 32 per cent! However, the Presidents, Vice-Presidents and unsuccessful candidates for the Presidency do not share this favourable situation. If we take the period since

[1] *Statistical Bulletin*, January 1968.

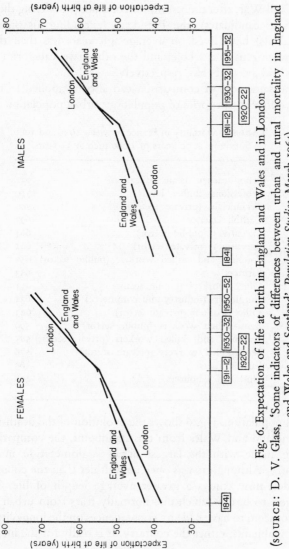

Fig. 6. Expectation of life at birth in England and Wales and in London

(SOURCE: D. V. Glass, 'Some indicators of differences between urban and rural mortality in England and Wales and Scotland', *Population Studies*, March 1964)

the Civil War, after the assumption of office (or offering themselves as candidates), the Presidents (excluding assassinated
Presidents) have lived on average 4·8 years less than their
fellow-citizens as a whole, and the other two categories 1·8
years and 4·0 years less, respectively.

The same sort of comparison can also be applied to two
very different categories of population: urban population and

TABLE 8. Mortality in France between 1955 and 1960.
Survivors at 70 years of 1,000 men at 35 years.

Schoolteachers (state education)	732
Professions, higher levels	719
Technicians (private sector)	700
Catholic clergy	692
Executives (public sector)	664
Executives (private sector)	661
Foremen and skilled workers (public sector)	653
Farmers	653
Office workers (public sector)	633
Employers (industry and commerce)	631
Office workers (private sector)	623
Semi-skilled workers (public sector)	590
Foremen and skilled workers (private sector)	585
Semi-skilled workers (private sector)	576
Farmworkers	565
Unskilled labourers	498

rural population. Fig. 6 shows the evolution of the death-rate
in England and Wales from this standpoint, the comparison
being made with the largest urban agglomeration in the
country. Although it was once unhealthier than the country,
London now enjoys a greater average length of life. The
dangers to health which one normally fears from urban life
do not seem to have had any consequences on the longevity of
the inhabitants, rather the contrary. It is really for the intense

period of industrialization of the last century that the picture of the town as a more deadly place than the country holds good (and in the past because of epidemics). The strong social differentiation in mortality during the last century is partly due to the deplorable conditions in which urbanization occurred. The results of a recent study undertaken in France repay examination. Between 1955 and 1960 about 50,000 employed men, divided into twelve socio-professional groups, were the subject of an investigation into mortality rates. The most important results are given in Table 8.

Thus, in general, a 35-year old teacher has 73 chances in 100 of living until 70, while an unskilled labourer has only 50.

The interpretation of these results is made easier by looking at the causes of death in the various social categories under examination.

Some diseases hit all professional categories with little variation: malignant tumours, cerebral vascular lesions and coronaries and other diseases of the heart. Other illnesses, on the other hand, hit the social groups in the survey with varying intensity: tuberculosis is particularly prevalent among unskilled labourers and more so in the private sector than in the public (better systems of detection); alcoholism and cirrhosis of the liver (one death in seven among unskilled and semi-skilled workers is from this cause); accidents, especially common in the working class.

These last three causes of death are themselves linked very closely, with alcoholism as the common denominator. According to the authors of the above study, 'the causes of death linked to alcoholism altogether account for between one-third and one-quarter of deaths among executives, technicians and office workers, and are responsible for half or more of deaths among farmworkers and unskilled labourers'.[1]

[1] G. Calot and M. Febvay, 'La mortalité différentielle suivant le milieu social', *Etudes et conjoncture*, no 11, November 1965).

It should be added that death by suicide is particularly frequent among farmworkers and unskilled labourers.

The arrangement of occupational groups according to level of mortality generally corresponds, then, to that of the prestige and income of these groups. But it would be an oversimplification to explain these cases of inequality in mortality solely by reference to economic status. There are exceptions, the most notable of which are schoolteachers and the Catholic clergy.

In fact, the cultural level of the different categories and the level of security they enjoy in the existing social organization play a fundamental part in this respect; very different types of life and attitudes to illness are determined by these two factors and these have enormous repercussions on the death-rate. It is remarkable that it should be the illnesses revealing one particular type of physical and mental distress which are the most unevenly divided, at least as causes of death. It is also striking that the less favoured categories suffer not only among their adult-members, but also among their children, as Table 9 shows.

Further, a quarter of the adult males in the population referred to could not be studied in respect of mortality rates; this was because the men concerned were too insufficiently integrated socially to permit statistical observation. Indirect observation suggests that this quarter of male adults has an even higher death-rate than the unskilled labourers. This group is composed of foreigners, unemployed, social misfits and people who have 'dropped out' of society for varying reasons. A new form of inequality has thus appeared in industrial society – that caused by the fluid character of a large unstable population, which has been unable to integrate itself into the existing social structure.

Insurance companies never ignore statistics and many of them offer special rates for certain occupational categories in car insurance and life assurance which are more advantageous than those for individual contracts.

This means that the general level of mortality of a population is closer to the level of the less-favoured categories than to that of the groups enjoying better living conditions, at least from the point of view of health.

TABLE 9. Infant and adult mortality in France (1959–60)

Socio-professional category	Infant mortality per 1,000	position	Adult mortality position
Top management	16·1	} 1	2
Professions	16·6		
Executives	18·1	2	3
Schoolteachers	18·5	3	1
Skilled workers and foremen	25·4	4	5
Farmers	27·5	5	4
Semi-skilled workers	29·4	6	6
Farmworkers	31·7	7	7
Unskilled workers	40·5	8	8

It is an inhuman characteristic of wealthy societies more or less to reject handicapped members who find it difficult to conform to the existing social framework. In this way, isolated areas of poverty are created which are not only material, but physical and moral. Social differences in mortality, which appeared at the dawn of industrialization, are thus far from disappearing.

Though interesting, these observations do not solve the problem of the causes of death. There are no trustworthy estimates of the influence of such factors as climate, diet and modes of life. The harmful effects of some habits (e.g. smoking and drinking) have been recognized; doubtless, too, some jobs are more dangerous than others, thus increasing the death-rate of those involved. These factors, however, are so closely linked that it is generally impossible to isolate the precise influence of each one. It is worth noting, for example, that the choice of occupation is partly determined by physical and mental condition. Some heavy jobs are only open to very robust individuals, while lighter jobs will attract weaker people. The effects of this selection process and the effects of the type of occupation can contradict each other, making it very difficult to interpret measurements of the death-rate. The analyst's task is made even more difficult if he has to take into consideration the numerous associations between individual characteristics, level of income, place of residence, level of intelligence and way of life. It has never been possible, for example, to assess the respective parts played by selection and living conditions in the excess mortality of those who do not marry as compared with married persons.

International comparisons are very useful in this sphere. In particular, it is remarkable that the average length of life in a country is not related to its economic development once a certain level (in fact, a fairly low one) has been reached. A comparison between the U.S.S.R. and the U.S.A. is extremely significant in this respect; the difference in life expectation between the two countries is minimal, while the purchasing power of the individual is probably four times greater in the latter. It is perhaps even more astonishing that infant mortality is higher in New York than Hong Kong.

Another 'privilege' of highly developed countries is the high level of excess mortality among men. Women usually live on average six to seven years longer than men, although it is generally agreed that the biological component of this phenomenon only gives the female an advantage of two years.

It would be just to say, however, that the most tangible sign of progress is the lengthening of life. Except in extraordinary circumstances (wars, political terror), the wishes of the individual coincide with the aims of society regarding the efforts to be made in this direction. However, ignorance of the part played by the different social factors and individual behaviour in the ageing of the human organism, prevents us from determining the best course to ensure the longest life. Furthermore, in our affluent societies, certain conflicts exist between individual desires and the attitudes which physical and psychological hygiene recommend.

The Social Effects of the Fall in Mortality

In modern societies, death is no longer present at the centre of life as it was for thousands of years. Fourastié has noted the consequences of this change on the development of family life:

At the end of the seventeenth century, the life of the average family man, married for the first time at 27, could be summed up thus: born into a family of five children, he had seen only half of them reach the age of 15; he himself had had five children of whom only two or three were alive at his death. . . .

This man, living on average until 52, will have seen about nine people die in his immediate family (not counting uncles, nephews and first cousins), among whom would have been one grandparent (the three others being dead before his birth), both his parents and three of his children. . . .

Nowadays. . . the situation of the average man of 50 is as follows: born into a family of three, at 26 he married a girl of 24. The only deaths he has seen have been those of his four grandparents. And he still has one chance in two of living a further 26 years. . . .

In the past, in one out of every two cases, the death of young children occurred before that of their father, and half the remaining children saw their father die before attaining their majority. The average age of the children at the death of their first parent was 14.

In the future, the 'average 'man will be 55 or 60 when his father dies. This means that the funds of the family inheritance will almost constantly be in the hands of men and women over 60; about half the private wealth of a nation will be in the hands of old people over 70.[1]

The author also adds that, in the past, men of 25 to 30 years old 'contracted unions which were only broken by death, but which usually lasted less than twenty years. Today, boys commit themselves in principle for life; but this time it will be for about fifty years.'

Because of the very high individual risks of death, the family unit of the past could only maintain itself if it was very extensive and included as many relatives as possible. The idea of the family restricted to father–mother–children was very vulnerable and not really viable, since the risk of the children becoming prematurely parentless was considerable.

The patriarchal family was thus a biological necessity and the break-up of this kind of family unit into the present restricted family cell as an independent unit is a direct result of the fall in mortality. Nowadays, when mortality is less, each individual coexists with a much larger number of his relatives, from whom, if we except young children, he lives separately. This loosening of family ties tends to lead to the isolation of old people who live away from their descendants with whom no economic links remain. Their means of subsistence, which used to be ensured by the extensive family unit, now depends on society as a whole – often a very precarious situation.

Finally, the fall in mortality could only result in a fall in fertility. With a high mortality rate as known by European couples in the sixteenth and seventeenth centuries, 50 per cent of the children brought into the world reached adolescence, which meant that the families which gave birth to six children

[1] Fourastié, 'De la vie traditionelle à la vie tertiaire', *Population*, July–September 1959.

(the average for the time) only brought up three or four. Given the present death rate, almost all the children would survive. This would result in unbearable educational costs and it is obviously sufficient for the modern couple to have a fertility rate only half that of couples in the past to achieve families of the same size.

There have been some attempts to analyse more precisely the connections between mortality and fertility, taking the essential motivation of the couple's fertility to be the wish to see a son surviving his parents, though it would doubtless be mistaken to imagine that couples could regulate their fertility with this end in mind with the imprecise information available. The conclusions reached by D. Heer and D. Smith are nevertheless very significant.[1] The aim of these two authors was to discover what fertility rate a married man would have to be sure that at least one of his sons would have 95 chances out of 100 of surviving him beyond his sixty-fifth birthday. With a life expectancy at birth of 20 years, the couple would need 10·4 live births; with life expectancy of 50 they would only need 5·5, and with 74 years only 1·9. Thus the complete replacement of generations could not be ensured with the low mortality in advanced industrialized countries, if a couple were simply content to have a male descendant who would survive until his father's sixty-fifth birthday. The same calculations by Heer and Smith show that the net reproduction rate aiming at the survival of a son is situated between 2·1 and 0·9 according to the level of mortality. There is, then, a clear dissociation, because of the variations possible in mortality, between the collective objective of ensuring the survival of the population (a reproduction rate under 1 would lead ultimately to the disappearance of a population) and the couple's aim of seeing one of its descendants survive the father to a fairly

[1] Cf. Contributed Papers, Sydney Conference, Australia, 21–25 August 1967, pp. 26–36.

advanced age. With an expectation of life of more than 73 years at birth, the pursuit of the second objective will prevent the realization of the first.

The interrelation of fertility and mortality also occurs at a more subtle level. Indeed, as soon as it appeared possible to protect human life effectively against death, life suddenly began to seem more precious. Considered, as Philippe Ariès puts it, as a field for treatment and no longer a battlefield for obscure forces, life has been more and more protected against external dangers, but at the same time it is given more grudgingly. The greater value placed on life has led to a greater value being placed on the child, and this has resulted in a concentration of effort on education, which, to be productive, demands considerable restrictions in numbers.

V

BIRTH CONTROL

As a means of limiting population, Malthus had only recommended late marriages and continence in marriage. Although he did know about the existence of other means of preventing birth, he only accepted preventive measures which did not involve what he called vice or misery.

These 'vicious' means had been known since antiquity. In his impressive *Medical History of Contraception*, Norman Himes starts his detailed survey of contraceptive methods with an exhaustive study of their use in primitive societies. Until the time of Malthus, contraception was only practised by restricted groups, particularly prostitutes; France, however, was something of an exception, having from the late eighteenth century a lower fertility rate, due to the fairly generalized practice of *coitus interruptus*. But it was left to the nineteenth century to try to rationalize attitudes to the subject and to bring the discussion out into the open.

Francis Place (1771–1854), a follower of Malthus, went much further in his conclusions than the master himself. His analysis of the inconvenience of high fertility and the advantages of voluntary limitation of births is even more relevant to the economic and social context of the time than the discussion of the subject in the *Principles of Population*. For instance Place writes in his *Diabolical Handbill*: 'When the number of working people in any trade or manufacture has for some years been too great, wages are reduced very low, and the working people become little better than slaves'. He also emphasizes 'the consequences of having more children than the income of the parents enables them to maintain and educate in a desirable manner.' This is, of course, a theme which present neo-Malthusians consider as one of their most important arguments.

But Place differs totally from Malthus when it comes to the choice of means of limiting births. He rejects the practice of late marriages because 'marriage in early life, is the only truly happy state, and if the evil consequences of too large family did not deter them, all men would marry while young and thus would many lamentable evils be removed from society.'

These observations led Francis Place to advise the use of contraceptives, which he described in his handbills: 'A piece of soft sponge about the size of a small ball attached to a very narrow ribbon and slightly moistened is introduced previous to sexual intercourse.'

Elsewhere, Place mentions *coitus interruptus*, but never the condom.

The *Illustrations and Proofs of the Principle of Population* by Place (1822) and what were later called the 'Diabolical Hand Bills' (by the same author, but published anonymously) form the social and ethical bases of the birth-control movement. After this beginning, the movement was to have considerable repercussions, first of all in the United States with the appearance of the *Fruits of Philosophy* by Charles Knowlton (1832), which is a descriptive presentation of the various contraceptive methods available. In England, *The Elements of Social Sciences* by George Drysdale (1854), which achieved widespread circulation through numerous translations, gave the neo-Malthusian movement its first real treatise on the various aspects of contraception: medical, economic and social. (Drysdale was, incidentally, the initiator of a Malthusian tradition.)

Neo-Malthusianism was well received by the greatest thinkers of the time, such as John Stuart Mill, and it achieved great publicity with the action in 1877 against Charles Bradlaugh and Annie Besant for having encouraged the London publication by Charles Watts of Knowltons's *Fruits of Philosophy*; in three months 125,000 copies were sold. Himes has called the period which begins with these events the democratization of birth control.

About thirty-five years later, the United States went through a similar phase at the time of that advocate of contraception, Margaret Sanger, a nurse in the poor districts of the East of New York. After an information-gathering visit to Europe, she began by publishing a lampoon, *Family Limitation*, and later a periodical, *The Woman Rebel*, in which she preached not only birth control but more generally the emancipation of women. In Brooklyn in 1916 she opened the first clinic in the United States for birth control advice.

At the same time as these advanced thinkers were engaged in their various struggles, birth control was benefiting from improvements in contraceptive techniques. Following the discovery of the process of vulcanization, the condom which had appeared in England in the eighteenth century, began to be manufactured in rubber during the second half of the nineteenth century. The safety of this method was thus increased, as the cost diminished. About 1880, Mensinga's vaginal diaphragm and the cervical cap and, a little later, chemical spermicides appeared. We can see that an increasingly scientific attitude to contraception was gradually developing.

Neo-Malthusianism, which started with Francis Place during Malthus's life-time, takes us a long way from the ideas and the methods recommended by the English parson. At the beginning of the twentieth century, the movement, particularly strong in England and the United States and helped along by various organizations, became increasingly active on the level of eugenics. An increasing amount of publicity began to be disseminated through birth-control clinics, the first one of which was opened in Holland in 1882. The idea of voluntary motherhood and fatherhood replaced purely restrictive ideas. To have the means of deciding the time of birth of one's children is one way to conjugal happiness though this presupposes that couples will have received some sexual education and marital advice.

After its phase of aggressive expansion, the neo-Malthusian movement became much more constructively accepted by the state and various religious bodies. The change of name in England in the thirties from 'National Birth Control Association' to 'Family Planning Association' is significant in this respect.

The evolution of neo-Malthusianism as an institution is inseparable from the changes in attitude towards it of governments and churches, the position of the latter often deciding the policy of the state.

In this respect, the position of the Catholic Church has always been restrictive, its doctrine being that 'The primary end of marriage is the procreation and the education of offspring; the secondary end, mutual aid and the remedying of concupiscence'. These principles, strongly reaffirmed by Pius XI in the Encyclical, *Casti Connubii* (1930), for a long time led the Catholic Church to reject all methods of contraception. Finally, the only method of birth control to be approved by the Church was the abstinence from sexual relations between husband and wife; periodical continence is thus the only permitted method of birth control. Even this is only permissible if it can be justified by 'sufficient and sure moral motives' (Pius XII).

In 1930, with the Declaration of the Lambeth Conference, the Anglican Church declared the use of contraception legitimate, not only by means of continence, but also by other methods, if justified by a healthy moral reason. Later statements have only confirmed and clarified this position, both at the 1958 Lambeth Conference and at the National Council of the Churches of Christ held in 1961 in theUnited States. It is especially noteworthy that no special restriction was imposed upon the latest means of contraception, the pill and the intra-uterine device.

This liberal attitude is obviously related to the legalization of organizations for the propagation of birth control or family planning in countries which are predominantly Protestant (Northern Europe and Anglo-Saxon countries). In contrast, the unbending attitude of Catholicism has been one of the factors, and sometimes the determining factor, in the rejection by some countries (Italy, Spain, etc.) of all educational schemes and publicity for promoting the techniques of birth control. Marxist opposition to the views of Malthus in communist countries has provoked widely differing attitudes to the problem of birth control; during the nineteenth century there was already disagreement among socialist thinkers on the subject. It should not be forgotten that Malthus attacked the utopian socialism of Condorcet, Godwin and Owen—opposition which was to continue with Proudhon and Fourier. It is especially at the end of the nineteenth century that divergent views appeared in the ranks of the socialists, especially among women supporters of socialism who, out of unwillingness to provide cannon fodder for the capitalists, advocated a childbearing strike. In addition, the anarchist movement, proclaiming sexual freedom and free love, favoured the spread of contraception.

In fact, in communist countries, attitudes towards population policies were to fluctuate from the greatest indifference (with a considerable increase in abortions) to the strictest anti-Malthusianism.

The short history of the ideas and institutions influencing birth control, outlined above, must not be confused with the evolution of mental attitudes and behaviour towards the limitation of births. If the development of neo-Malthusianism as a doctrine and technique has played a part in the fall in the birth-rate, as it obviously has, this fall could have occurred quite independently of the awareness of the various problems raised by the advocates of birth control. In this respect, the example of France is extremely interesting.

There are numerous pointers which indicate a beginning of a voluntary limitation of births in France during the eighteenth century, thus practising neo-Malthusianism before Malthus. We have, first of all, the testimony of certain writers, such as Moheau who, in 1756, reckoned 'that even in the villages, nature is cheated'. Even Mirabeau, in 1756, remarks, 'Nature must be horrified at the methods dictated by good living to avoid the embarrassment of a large family'. In this way then, practices which were first of all only used in the context of extra-marital relations and sexual irregularity, gradually spread into marital relations. Mirabeau seems to have been correct in his criticism of good living. In a study of the dukes and peers of the Ancien Régime in France and of the bourgeoisie in Geneva, Louis Henry has found statistical evidence of a perceptible limitation of fertility from the seventeenth century onwards. The same author also finds unmistakable traces of a drop in the birth rate in rural France in the second half of the eighteenth century, thus confirming Moheau's opinion.

These observations are interesting because they show that a dissociation can exist between the level of contraceptive technique of a population and the demographic effectiveness of that technique. At the time, the French had at their disposal only *coitus interruptus*, an unpleasant and by no means infallible method. However, the effect of this method on a national scale has been quite appreciable; it is thus possible for an attitude towards the limitation of births to develop without special propaganda being undertaken.

Neo-Malthusianism, which found its theorists and promoters in England, was practised among the French peasantry long before Malthus and Francis Place.

Today, the status of birth control in the world varies enormously from country to country. If we confine ourselves entirely to industrialized countries, we can encounter both the greatest tolerance and the greatest restriction.

England and the United States, where the neo-Malthusian movement was born, together with the countries of Northern Europe, are the most advanced in accepting the existence of organizations for the dissemination of information, not only on contraception, but also on such related matters as sexual education and the physical and moral problems which go with marriage. In the United States, the American Birth Control League, started by Margaret Sanger in 1921 and renamed the Planned Parenthood Federation of America in 1942, with branches in over a hundred towns, is responsible for the greater part of contraceptive advice in the country, At the same time it advises on such problems as sterility and, through specialist branches, has even undertaken research into human fertility. In Great Britain, the Family Planning Association of Great Britain, started in 1930, is the most active organization and benefits considerably from the very co-operative attitude of the British medical profession. An international organization, the International Planned Parenthood Federation, founded in 1952 in New Delhi, represents about forty countries and has its headquarters in London.

In strict contrast, France, where advocates of neo-Malthusianism such as Paul Robin were very active at the beginning of the century, has remained almost untouched by most of the most recent developments in the spread of the ideas and practice of planned parenthood. This state of affairs can be explained by the existence until 1968 of the law of 1920 which forbade all publicity in favour of contraception. It is open to question, however, whether this law, passed after the severe losses in manhood of the First World War, halted the fall in the birth rate in France. The question remains open to debate and forms part of the much larger problem of the relationships existing between the free dissemination of contraceptive information and contraceptive devices, the level of fertility, and the number of abortions.

For instance, it is very difficult to come to any clear conclusion on the role played by contraception in removing the justification for abortion. The main objection against this interpretation of the function of contraception is that most contraceptives are inconvenient and can fail because of negligence or ineptitude in use, and that accidental pregnancies resulting from such failure seem peculiarly destined to end in abortion. Apart from this, abortion is likely to be accepted more readily in the climate of free choice in which conceptions can occur when information on birth control is made freely available, than when the whole subject of procreation is surrounded with official restrictions.

It seems very probable, however, that a policy of encouraging the spread of information on the means of avoiding unwanted pregnancies will slow down the rate of abortions, especially at the present time when very efficient contraceptives are available. If it is impossible to draw any definite conclusions in this sphere, it is because direct observation is virtually precluded.

For similar reasons, the connections between the level of fertility and the level of dissemination of information on contraception are difficult to assess. We noted, for instance, in France in the eighteenth century that these two variables could be independent of one another, contraception having achieved some currency without elaborate methods being available and clearly without any attempts to influence public opinion in its favour. More recently a number of contradictory examples have been noted. The only conclusion that can be drawn, as is the case with most social phenomena, is that there is no immutable dependence in time and space between the different variables in question.

An important new factor has been the appearance over the past few years of two new contraceptives, easy to use and almost completely effective: the pill and the intra-uterine

TABLE 10. Contraceptive methods used in the United States

Methods	1933–34	1955	1965
Condom	24·4	26	18
Diaphragm	3·4	24	10
Rhythm	*	21	13
Douche	25·8	7	6
Withdrawal	29·0	7	5
Other methods	17·4	15	24
Pill	—	—	24
Total	100	100	100

* Included in 'Other methods'; does not seem to have been more than 2 per cent
SOURCES: 1933–34: results given by N. Himes in *Medical History of Contraception*, p. 345.
   1955: Freedman, Whelpton and Campbell, *Family Planning, Sterility and Population Growth*, 1959.
   1965: *National Fertility Study.*

device (I.U.D.). This technical development, together with the existence of a public better informed on contraception, has led to changes in the frequency of use of the different methods. These changes are especially marked in the countries which enjoy the greatest freedom in the matter and, in this respect, the United States presents the most interesting example of the evolution of habits (see Table 10). The years between 1933–34 and 1955 are marked by the disappearance of the more primitive means (douche, withdrawal) and, with a more knowledgeable public, the increasing use of more elaborate techniques, the diaphragm and periodical abstinence, the means authorized by the Catholic Church. By 1965, the use of the pill has already become widespread (the I.U.D. had only only appeared in the preceding year). No method made known through education in contraception is used as much as the pill, which has established itself at the expense of two other techniques, the diaphragm and periodic abstinence.

TABLE II. United States: number of Catholics conforming with Church doctrine on contraception

Date	Practising Catholics		Total
	regular	irregular	
1955	78%	53%	70%
1960	69%	35%	62%
1965	56%	26%	47%

SOURCE: Charles F. Westoff and Norman B. Ryder, 'United States: Methods of Fertility Control 1955, 1960 and 1965', *Studies in Family Planning*, February 1967.

The behaviour of Catholics is of interest in this respect. As we saw above, the Catholic Church only permits the practice of periodic abstinence or no contraception at all. In 1965, this ruling was observed by less than half the total number of members of the Church, while ten years ago 70 per cent behaved according to the official doctrine. The advent of the pill only encouraged this changing attitude and induced uncertainty in the Catholic hierarchy (a tendency sharply halted by the Encyclical, *Humanae Vitæ*); in this example, behaviour is related to degree of religious practice (see Table II).

The choice of contraceptive methods by household depends on numerous other criteria than religious ones. More precisely, if there are perceptible differences in behaviour between various religious groups, then their origin does not lie exclusively in the observance of religious precepts, which, except in the case of Catholicism, are not very strict. In fact, it is socio-cultural characteristics, allied to religious persuasion, which are responsible for certain differences. In the United States, the use of the most rational method (condom) and the trickiest method (diaphragm) is more widespread among Jews than among other religious groups. It follows, too, that what is applicable to religious groups of the country can also explain differences between countries, which can depend too an the varying status accorded to the idea of birth control.

Other criteria which probably influence most couples in their choice of a method are cost, facility of usage and effectiveness. This latter consideration has always been something of a worry to advocates of contraception, in their anxiety to find the best methods in this respect and thus spread the principle of birth control. But, apart from the up-to-date and totally safe (pill) or the nearly safe (I.U.D.) methods, it can be said that the efficiency of a technique depends more on the couple using it and their motivation, than on the technique itself; this is especially applicable in the case of elaborate methods, such as the condom, diaphragm and periodic abstinence.

Since the possibilities of reproduction of the human couple are so considerable and mortality so low as to allow most newly-born infants to reach adulthood, contraception appears to be an absolute necessity for modern families. Otherwise families would reach such dimensions that the expansion rates of populations would become intolerable. Contraception is practised in most developed countries, with varying degrees of facility of access to the different methods, according to social milieu and current legislation.

Birth control is now more than a form of behaviour for

limiting family size. By regulating human fertility, it not only ensures the birth of no more than the number of children desired, but also regulates the length of time between births, thereby permitting the genuine planning of a family. Yet two-thirds of humanity are still unwilling to accept the techniques which permit such planning.

VI

DIFFERENTIAL FERTILITY

HUMAN fertility is regulated by both biological and psycho-social factors.

By following the stages leading to the birth of a child, Kingsley Davis and Judith Blake have isolated three categories of variables:

intercourse variables (formation and dissolution of marriages, especially frequency of marriages and age at marriage, divorces, widowhood, remarriages and the frequency of sexual intercourse);

conception variables (fecundity of couples, use of contraceptives);

gestation variables (foetal mortality, voluntary or not).

The intervention of so many variable factors means that fertility can vary considerably for different populations. Indeed, restricting ourselves to national populations, the annual birth rate per 1,000 inhabitants may fluctuate from 60 to a figure as low as 12. We can gain a further idea of the range of possible situations by comparing the average number of children of a married woman, for a given age at marriage, in conditions of natural fertility (absence of birth control) and in a population practising birth control. The examples given below refer, on the one hand, to what may be regarded as the average level of natural fertility (mean of situations observed among ancient European populations and the populations of contemporary developing countries) and, on the other, the present French population.

Women married at	Average number of live births per woman remaining married until at least 50		
	in conditions of natural fertility	in France now	reduction
20 years	8·4	3·4	60%
25 "	6·3	2·5	60%
30 "	4·2	1·8	57%
35 "	2·4	1·2	50%
40 "	0·9	0·5	44%

Thus, deliberate efforts to reduce natural fertility can lead to a reduction in fertility of about 45 to 60 per cent.

Natural Fertility and Differential Fertility

In the absence of conscious efforts to limit the number of births, birth-rate and fertility levels tend to fluctuate. The information presented in the table gives us some idea of an average situation, from which actual situations can vary appreciably. Thus L. Henry, assembling the results for various populations not practising birth control, finds that the total fertility of women married at 20 and remaining so until at least the age of 50 varies from 6·2 to 10·9 (compared to our preceding average rate of 8·4). The birth rates, then, can vary between 40 and 60 per 1,000.

The differences in fertility in the absence of birth control can depend on the time and frequency of marriage, on the variations in the length of the breast-feeding period (causing temporary sterility), on the health of the population and possibly also on the frequency and gravity of venereal diseases. The most obvious consequence of this differentiation in conditions of natural fertility is the very variable demographic dynamism of the populations concerned. For example, in ancient Europe, because of late marriages and the high proportion of people who remained single, the birth rate was never as high as it is now in some developing countries; it is generally reckoned to have been about 40 per 1,000 in the first case and frequently between 45 and 55 per 1,000 in the second.

Differences in the ability to conceive of different populations, ethnic groups or individuals are also worth attention; there is, after all, no doubt about the existence of such differences. It has been possible in this way to determine the frequency of conceptions at each menstrual cycle for women who do not practise birth control (this frequency is called *fecundability*). This frequency is partly determined by the couple's biological capacity for reproduction and usually varies from 10 to 30 per cent. Information on the same subject has been obtained in a completely different way: during inquiries in the United States in 1955 and 1960 among married women aged 18–40, it was discovered that almost a third could be classed as sub-fecund, in view of the fact that they found it difficult or even impossible to have children at the time of the inquiry.

To end these considerations on the biological aspects of fertility, it is worth mentioning that there seems to be a positive correlation between the ability to have children and longevity. This is supported by the fact, observed on several occasions in different groups of married women, that the sample of women who lived for longer than 70 years had a higher fertility rate than those who died between the ages of 50 and 70

Birth Control and Differential Fertility

On the question of differential fertility, the part played by voluntary behaviour in the matter of procreation, i.e. birth control, is extremely interesting.

Practised by nearly all couples in the economically developed countries, birth control will soon be a necessity all over the world. The physiological potential of the human species for reproduction is considerable (doubling of the population in fifteen years), owing to the reduction in the mortality rate (which will diminish still further in the future). This makes the study of the spread of birth control even more interesting.

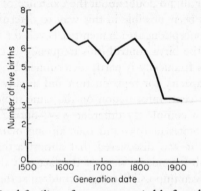

Fig. 7. Total fertility of women married before the age of
25 in the British nobility
(SOURCE: T. H. Hollingsworth, *The Demography of the
British Peerage*)

In modern times, it was in France that a sufficiently large proportion of the population first practised contraception to the extent of influencing the overall birth rate of the country: around 1800 the birth rate had already fallen to 31 per 1,000, while the figure was probably 35 per 1,000 in England. It was only after 1850 that the other, more developed European countries were to follow this movement. Between the two wars, the situation became more or less comparable in these countries, the birth rate fluctuating between 15 and 20 per 1,000 inhabitants.

Changes within a single population are the result of the

spread of birth control habits through the various social groups. But, in this context, each of these social groups has its own history, and the differences which can be observed between them, at any given date, result from the differences in time at which the development of birth control practice has taken place and even perhaps from differences in the rhythm with which these changes have happened.

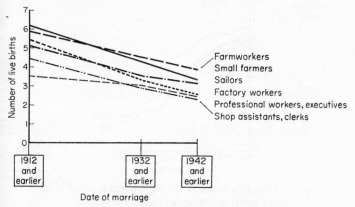

Fig. 8. Fertility in Norway by socio-occupational category of the husband, based on the population censuses of 1930, 1950 and 1960

The data on the British aristocracy are interesting from this point of view (see Fig. 7): between 1550 and 1700 there was a significant fall in the birth rate, although, very probably, nothing similar took place among the rest of the population at that time. In the eighteenth century there is a period of slight growth (this is perhaps true for the whole of the country where the records suggest an increase of 10 to 20 per cent). For the women born after 1800, the fall is very sudden, while, on a national scale, this movement is only really appreciable for the generations born after 1850.

Hence, as far as the limitation of births is concerned, the British aristocracy was in the forefront, as were the dukes and peers of France and the bourgeoisie of Geneva.

The example of Norway is even more striking, because here it is possible to see, across the different socio-occupational groups, the movement towards increasingly widespread control of fertility (see Fig. 8). In this example, observation of

Fig. 9. Fertility in Norway among women married at 24–25 years, according to place of residence

the movement commences when differences between groups is already very great (fertility of marriages before 1912, observed in 1930). In the latest observations (marriages before 1942, observed in 1960) we can see that the fall in fertility has continued uninterrupted, the differences between the groups diminishing slightly. A similar sort of development can be observed in Fig. 9, again for Norway, where the difference is according to place of residence, urban or rural.

Faced with this sort of development, demographers for long imagined that, in future, human fertility would inevitably tend towards a very low level and that the groups who remained relatively fertile would, in the long run, follow in the steps of those who were more advanced in voluntary restriction. As we shall see, the demographic history of the last twenty years has invalidated these views.

Factors in Differential Fertility

If one lists the characteristics of individuals to be considered as exemplifying the differences in fertility in a population, one is faced with such an imposing number that the problem is left almost untouched: what factors do explain the differences in behaviour regarding fertility? All the characteristics in question are to be found more or less closely connected in the same individual and it is impossible to determine which have the determining influence; farmers are only found in rural districts, certain religious categories are particularly well-represented in certain social groups, better educated people are also those with the highest income and so on. The ideal solution is to study how much fertility varies according to one single characteristic, when all other variables have been controlled. For instance, the variation of fertility by religious affiliation can be studied in a group where all members have the same income, same place of residence and same profession. Unfortunately, this method breaks the population up into a large number of sub-groups which are too small for any statistical examination to be significant.

However, even if we cannot determine the deepest causes of the differences in reproduction, it is at least possible to define some essential and permanent features of differential fertility in Western countries.

One of the most constant factors in differential fertility is place of residence. Urbanization is always linked to low fertility, simply because urban conditions are less favourable for bringing up a family (see Fig. 9, which shows this pheno-menon in Norway). In towns, the possibilities of social advancement and mobility are greater, the differentiation o society sharper and the diffusion of ideas and cultural movements more intense. All these conditions are favourable to a

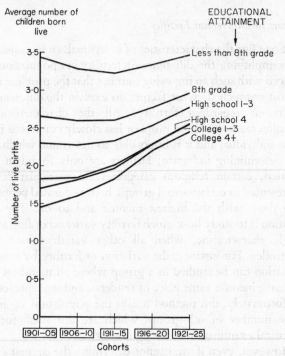

Fig. 10. United States: Estimated number of children ever born per 1,000 women by the end of the childbearing period, for ever-married white women by educational attainment

(SOURCE: Arthur A. Campbell, 'Recent Fertility Trends in the United States and Canada', World Population Conference, Belgrade, 30 August–10 September 1965)

more rational attitude towards human life and, especially, towards the way in which it is brought into existence.

Level of income, social level and cultural level are usually negatively correlated with the level of fertility. As we observed before, this is partly because these three variables are closely linked. The differentiation of fertility according to these variables is not necessarily permanent. The upper classes (and consequently the wealthier and better-educated) were the first to restrict their fertility and it is this early use of birth control which caused, for a long time, the almost perfect negative correspondence between social level and level of fertility: a falling level of fertility corresponded to a rise in social level. But, if we take the situation as it has been for several decades, we find that a continually falling fertility rate among the lower classes is paralleled by a rise at the top of the social scale: thus the range of variation has been reduced. In some populations an even more radical change has been observed, with a rise in fertility appearing in all classes. Such a situation may be seen in the United States if married women are classified by educational level. Fig. 10 shows that the fall in fertility in the less educated classes continued until the generations born around 1910, after which a moderate rise occurred. Among the more educated categories the rise started with the generations born around 1900, or even earlier, and has been much more appreciable. It should be mentioned, too, that the better-educated classes of the population had gone much further in the direction of voluntary infertility than the less-educated classes: the average number of live births in this latter category has never dropped below 3·2, while it appears to have reached the very low limit of 1·4 in the former. Here, too, it is possible to see a narrowing range of variation: from 1·44 to 3·42 around 1900 (that is, from 1 to 2·37), but from 2·45 to 3·47 around 1920 (that is, from 1 to 1·42).

Religious affiliation accounts for some of the visible differences in fertility, but no hard and fast rules can be drawn up regarding its influence. In countries where several religious groups coexist, there is a hierarchy of fertility which looks more or less constant; in this respect the information we have on Holland and the United States repays examination (see Table 12).

Although Westoff, Potter and Sagi could write, on the basis of their inquiry, the *Princeton Fertility Study*, that 'religious preference, that is, preference for the Protestant, Catholic

TABLE 12. Fertility according to religion

Holland		United States	
Catholics	4·62	Catholics	2·56
Reformed Church	3·05	Protestants	2·38
Calvinists	4·13	Jews	1·81
No religion	2·48	No religion*	2·51
		* or religion not given	
Total fertility after 21–25 years of marriage in 1960, by the religion of the woman (existing first marriages, all ages at time of marriage).		Total fertility by woman aged 45–49 years, currently married, in 1957.	
SOURCE: D. Glass, 'Fertility Trends in Europe, since the Second World War,' *Population Studies*, March 1968, p. 126.		SOURCE: *Current Population Survey*, 1957.	

or Jewish faith, is the strongest of all major social characteristics in its influence on fertility[1]', the whole matter is much more complex than this. The intervention of other variables shows after all that the influence of religion varies according to sub-group, so much so that, in some social strata, this influence does not figure at all. Table 13 shows, for example, the relative

[1] *The Third Child*, p. 238.

level of fertility of Catholics (in relation to Protestants) in West Germany according to size of locality of residence.[1] Closer analysis shows that the influence of religion declines when there is an increase in the influence of the place of residence.

Another noteworthy attempt to explain this phenomenon is that by Lincoln M. Day.[2] According to him – and the statistical evidence he produces is very convincing – the higher

TABLE 13. West Germany. Births to Catholic women, per 100 births to Protestant women. (Basic data: births per 1,000 marriages in each category.)

Locality of	Marriages in 1920 and before	Marriages from 1937 to 1940
Less than 2,000 inhabitants	130	110
From 2,000 to 99,999 inhabitants	128	105
More than 100,000 inhabitants	116	100

fertility level among Catholics only occurs when they constitute a minority group in a country (United Kingdom, Holland, Switzerland, United States). When they occupy the position of a majority group they often have a low fertility level, and this level may even be lower than that of non-Catholics in the countries where Catholics hold a dominant position (France, Belgium, Italy, Austria).

The increase in fertility in several countries of western Europe, which happened generally during the forties, was a

[1] cf. K. Schwarz, 'Nombre d'enfants suivant le milieu physique et social en Allemagne occidentale', Population, January-February, 1965.

[2] 'Natality and Ethnocentrism', Population Studies, March 1968.

considerable surprise for demographers. If we analyse this increase by social category, we find a rise in fertility in the groups which formerly had the lowest levels, accompanied by a slowing down in the fall in fertility among very fertile groups, although, here again, there was a distinct rise in some cases. It remains, however, that the phenomenon of differential fertility has become somewhat less important. This tendency towards greater uniformity in fertility should be seen in a wider context: there is an increasingly definite consensus of opinion as to what the modern family should be and there are more and more efficient means of contraception which allow the couple to modify fertility in accordance with their wishes regarding the size of their family. The growing uniformity of levels of living and the relative security of the populations of industrialized countries (low unemployment, social provisions against illness, education facilities) have reduced the fears of having to bring up a child. All this very probably explains the rising fertility level in all classes of society.

Various Consequences

The progressive extension of the practice of limiting the size of the family has had the effect, among others, of causing the endogamy rate (the probability of marrying a blood relative) among populations to rise temporarily.

This relatively unexpected result has only been felt and established recently by the discovery of the rising percentage of consanguineous marriages at the end of the nineteenth century in two French departments, Loir-et-Cher and Finistère and, to a lesser degree, in a number of Italian dioceses[1]. Thus, in Loir-et-Cher, consanguineous marriages went up

* Cf. Sutter: 'Fréquence de l'endogamie et ses facteurs au 19me siècle', *Population*, March–April 1968.

from 2–3 per cent of all marriages at the beginning of the nineteenth century to more than 5 per cent just before 1900, only
to fall to 0·5 per cent today. One of the mechanisms contribu-
ting to this increase seems to have been the following. During
the phase of expansion of birth control, the situation differed
greatly from family to family; some were already closely
limiting their fertility, while others still had a purely physiological fertility; this led to great heterogeneity of the number
of children by family and to the rapid demographic domination by some families of small geographical areas where most
marriages took place. In other words, the proportion of
related people in a community rises considerably when a
substantial proportion of families practise birth control, leaving
others to see to the continued survival of the population and
to eventual demographic expansion. In such an unbalanced
population, the chances of marriage between cousins are appreciably higher.

Let us now consider the results of the differences in degree of
family limitation among the various groups of the population
of one country. These differences can lead to considerable
variations in the demographic vitality of these groups.
Consequently, the distribution of a population by some
characteristics (ethnic, religious) can be modified by different
fertility characteristics. There are many present-day examples
to illustrate this: the higher fertility level of the Flemish
population accentuates the preponderance of this group in the
total population of Belgium; the difference between sizes of
the Jewish and Arab populations of Israel is constantly diminishing because of the low fertility rate of the former as opposed
to the natural fertility of the latter; almost everywhere the
fertility of Catholics is higher than that of other religious or
non-religious groups, and the demographic pre-eminence of
the former tends to increase.

Geneticists and biologists have long been interested in these differences in fertility between sub-groups of a given population, first because of an almost universal negative correlation between intelligence and fertility, and secondly, because of the largely hereditary nature of intelligence. Logically, such phenomenon implies an increasing demographic domination by the less intelligent classes and is thus a grave menace to the evolution of humanity. Lorimer and Osborn, in their *Dynamics of Population* (1934) have expressed this fear for the United

TABLE 14. Average Intelligence Quotients of public school children classified by size of family

Class of family by number of children reported	Average I.Q. of children in each class
1	117
2	118
3	114
4	108
5	106
6	106
7	105
8	103
9 and over	98

SOURCE: Lorimer and Osborn, *Dynamics of Population*, p. 196.

States in no uncertain terms: '... at present the negative association between fertility and cultural-intellectual level in the population of the United States reveals a powerful force that is working against our most cherished national ideals and that threatens to defeat the aims of the whole public education movement. If this force remains unchecked, its eventual political and social repercussions may be tremendous.'

It was this type of thinking and the fear of racial degeneration which led to the eugenics movement of the end of the nineteenth and the beginning of the twentieth century.

The first empirical denial of these purely intellectual deductions came with the findings of the famous Scottish inquiry of 1932 and 1947 into all 11 year old children. In 15 years the intelligence quotient for that age had *increased* by 2 points, that is, about 4 points between two generations, at a time when certain people had been talking of an average *loss* of 4 points.

Such a reversal of evidence must lead us to reconsider the arguments upon which previous pessimistic forecasts were based. The alarmist conclusions of Lorimer and Osborn seemed to be strongly supported by Table 14. And Sir Cyril Burt, for his part, in his report to the Royal Commission on Population, gives the following findings:

I.Q.	Average number of children in family
over 130	2·3
115–130	2·7
100–115	3·3
85–100	3·6
70–85	4·2
under 70	4·7

Although impressive, these findings do not necessarily imply a higher rate of expansion among the less intelligent classes of society. Other factors play a part in determining this rate: frequency of marriages, frequency of infertile marriages and length of life. No inquiry so far carried out at a given time on any group of children has been able to take all these factors into account.

This is where the superiority of longitudinal investigations is shown, where the total history of a group is studied; in favour of this type of investigation, Bajema has been able to show[1] that individuals of low I.Q. married less often, that

[1] *Eugenics Quarterly*, December 1963.

many of those who married were almost totally infertile, and also that their average life was measurably shorter.

Taking all these factors into account, it is the adolescents with the highest I.Q. who have the highest rate of reproduction and the group with the lowest intelligence (I.Q. lower than 80) which reproduces least successfully. It must be added that the same author has established a system of classification

TABLE 15. Intelligence of parents and children classified according to fathers' occupations

Occupational category	Average Intelligence Quotient	
	Children	Adults
Higher professional: Administrative	120·3	153·2
Lower professional: Technical Executive	114·6	132·4
Highly skilled: clerical	109·7	117·1
Skilled	104·5	108·6
Semi-skilled	98·2	97·5
Unskilled	92·0	96·8
Casual	89·1	81·6
Institutional	67·2	57·3

SOURCE: *Papers of the Royal Commission on Population*, Vol. V, Memoranda presented to the Royal Commission, p. 55.

analogous to Table 14 and has verified his own previous findings by it. This simply goes to underline the ineptitude of such analysis to account for differential reproduction according to intelligence quotient. More generally, this apparent paradox shows the difficulty and importance of correct quantitative analyses in demography. Much literature which claims to take demographic factors into account is full of erroneous conclusions because of incorrect statistical analysis.

The hypothesis of the hereditary nature of intelligence was

also considered in the argument which concluded that differential fertility does cause the intellectual impoverishment of populations. Still on this subject, Cyril Burt, again in his report to the Royal Commission on Population, produced the impressive Table 15, which also includes the parents' socio-professional category

In fact, except in particular cases, it has never been possible to separate the genetic factor and the environmental factor in the definition of intelligence. The question of transmission of intelligence in a population under the influence of differential fertility has never been totally answered. It can be said, however, that the pessimistic views of some geneticists and biologists on the future of human intelligence are not supported by the direct measurements of recent trends.

VII

THE MODERN FAMILY

Now reduced to father, mother and children, the modern family is also characterized by the small number of children born. But almost all these children now survive, so that the size of the family expressed in terms of the number of surviving children is not really inferior to that in times of high fertility, but which were also times of high mortality.

The family is affected by a number of events which it is worth studying in themselves before we examine their significance in the context of the household: age at and frequency of marriage, importance of widowhood and divorce, and the importance of extra-marital conceptions and births.

Nuptiality in western Europe is characterized by late and relatively less frequent marriages. This explains why, even before any attempt at voluntary limitation of births, the birth rate was lower there than that observed today in developing countries.

The recent evolution of nuptiality is marked by a tendency towards earlier and more frequent marriages. This is the conclusion reached by Ryder in the United States, where 91 per cent of the women and 88 per cent of the men of the 1870–75 generations married, compared with 96 per cent and 92 per cent respectively of the 1925–30 generation. At the same time, the average age at the time of first marriage in the same groups changed from 23·4 to 21·4 for the women, and from 27·1 to 24·3 for the men.

However, there is still an appreciable contrast between

western Europe and the developing countries. In the former it is rare for more than 90 per cent of the men and women to marry (in extreme cases, such as Ireland, only 70 to 80 per cent do so, because of peculiarities in the demo-economic history of the country), while in the latter, proportions of 95 to 100 per cent are frequent .While the average age at time of

TABLE 16. United States. Average age at marriage according to level of education. White population in 1940
and 1950.

		Educated people		Uneducated people
		Maximum*	Minimum	
Men	1940	27·7 years	24·7 years†	27·5 years
	1950	25·7 years	23·3 years‡	27·1 years
Women	1940	25·4 years	21·4 years§	25·3 years
	1950	23·2 years	19·9 years§	23·9 years

* Have reached level of 'college, 4 years or more'.
†   "   "   "   " 'grammar school, 1–4 years'.
‡   "   "   "   " 'high school, 1–3 years'.
§   "   "   "   " 'grammar school, 5–8 years'.
SOURCE: C. Tietze and P. Lauriat, 'Age at marriage and education attainment in U.S.A.' *Population Studies*, November 1955.

the first marriage is between 20 and 24 for women in western Europe, it is generally around 20 in the Third World.

Relatively little is known about the differences in this connection between the social classes of a particular society, although late marriages have been a mark of the upper classes for a long time. If we look at the data in Table 16 covering the influence of education on the age at marriage in the United States, it looks as though this situation remains unchanged. These findings show, however, that the distance between extreme groups has tended to diminish (the difference between maxima and minima has fallen from 3 to 2·4 years for men and from 4 to 3·3 for women), which is one of the aspects of the tendency towards uniformity of demographic behaviour. The study of the formation of the family offers us many examples of this. The special part played by persons who have received no education and whose degree of social integration is uncertain, should not be forgotten; their age at marriage is higher than that of any other group.

Marriage can be broken either by the death of one of the spouses, or by divorce. The effects in the family of these two events as of subsequent remarriage can be considerable.

We have seen how the fall in mortality has changed the circumstances in which families live. From our point of view it is the substantial disappearance of orphans at an early age, resulting from this fall, which is especially important. Within the space of twenty-five years, the proportion of married people under 50 who have lost their spouse has fallen by more than 60 per cent. Nowadays, in western Europe, it is more usual for a child to be deprived of one of its parents through voluntary separation than through death.

In most countries, the break-up of marriage can be legally validated; in any case, the statistician can only analyse those separations which are legalized. Although it does not give a complete picture of the phenomenon, the use of statistics on divorces in countries where they are legally acceptable, allows us to follow its evolution and to make some comparison between countries (though differences in legislation may be the cause of differences in the number of legal separations). The tendency is towards a more or less constant rise of the divorce rate, with the rate of broken marriages ranging from 8 per cent in England and Wales and 10 per cent in France, to 20 per cent in some socialist countries (Rumania, Hungary), and to 25 per cent in the United States.

In western societies, fertility is essentially legitimate fertility. The state of *mores* leads to varying situations according to country. Low in certain countries (3 per cent in Italy and Belgium, 6 per cent in France), rather high in others (15 per cent in Sweden in 1967), the proportion of illegitimate births does not appear to depend on easily explicable factors, such as religion, or even the sexual and contraceptive education of the population. Though in most countries the relative frequency of illegitimate births varies relatively little in time, there is a

TABLE 17. Ratio of illegitimate to total live births (illegitimate births per 100 live births)

Year	White	Non–White	Year	White	Non–White
1940	2·0	16·8	1955	1·9	20·2
1945	2·4	17·9	1960	2·3	21·6
1950	1·8	18·0	1965	4·0	26·3

SOURCE: Center for Health Statistics, *Vital Statistics for the United States*, 1965.

visible tendency towards a rise in certain cases. This has happened in the United States where there is a considerable difference between the white and black populations (see Table 17).

An even more revealing phenomenon is open to investigation by the demographer: the proportion of illegitimate conceptions, at least those not terminated by induced abortion. These conceptions appear to represent most frequently between one-third (in France, for instance) and two-thirds (in Sweden) of first conceptions. In the case of illegally induced abortions, it is impossible to know their number and, more particularly, to measure the influence of legislation on contraception in this field. We have already seen that the number of illegitimate conceptions does not seem to depend on the degree to which a population knows about contraception; this may be the case with induced abortions as well. It remains to be added, however, that, in the United States, the proportion of these abortions is estimated at 5 to 25 per cent in relation to births.

The Family Cycle

To place these events in the context of the family cycle in order to establish the typology of the modern family is not

TABLE 18. U.S.A. The family life cycle for women born
from 1880 to 1889

	Year of birth (birth cohort) of women					
	1880 to 1889	1890 to 1899	1900 to 1909	1910 to 1919	1920 to 1929	1930 to 1939
First marriage	21·6	21·4	21·1	21·7	20·8	19·9
Birth of first child	22·9	22·9	22·6	23·7	23·0	21·5
Median years marriage to birth of first child	1·5	1·4	1·5	1·7	1·6	1·3
Birth of last child	32·9	31·1	30·4	31·5	30·0–31·0	(NA)
Median years first marriage to the birth of last child	11·3	9·7	9·3	9·8	9·2–10·2	(NA)
Completed fertility	3·4	2·8	2·5	2·5	3·1	(NA)

SOURCE: P. Glick and R. Parke, 'New Approaches in Studying the Life Cycle of the Family', *Demography*, 1965, Vol. II.

easy. The phenomena cannot be fully described by reference to average situations and we must necessarily go into the details of the various possible individual cases.

P. Glick who, in the United States, tried to incorporate

demographic characteristics into individual statistical histories, has succeeded in finding a mode of description which, though schematic, very usefully stresses the important features of the contemporary family, which have been defined following the work of Fourastié.

Table 18 outlines certain essential stages in the make-up of a family. The generations in question are all greatly given to family limitation, the total fertility of the married women ranging somewhere between 2·5 and 3·4 children.

This fertility is usually achieved within a few years, often the first ten years of marriage. The woman thus reaches the age of thirty, having had all her children. This contrasts with the situation in a traditional society, where fertility would be about 6 or 7 live births, the woman being about 40 at the last birth.

If we turn from the generation of 1880 to the generation of 1940, the changes are numerous: earlier marriage, fertility declining and then rising appreciably, shortening of the child-bearing period and a shorter time between marriage and first birth.

Thus, the birth of children to a family occupies a more and more limited phase, leaving the woman free for other tasks at a much earlier age. Since life has been considerably lengthened, the modern woman has an expectation of life of several decades after having given birth to her children and brought them up (in establishing the time of marriage of the last child of the couple as being when the mother has just passed 50, Glick shows us that she can still hope to survive the departure of the last-born by thirty years).

The making of the family, then, although still an important part of a couple's life in our time and in our industrialized societies, is a more and more restricted episode. This is because, first, children are borne earlier and within a shorter period of married life, and secondly, as a result of increased human longevity. The life of an indvidual can be roughly divided into three phases of comparable length: childhood and youth, parental life, and post-parental life.

Planned Childbirth

To parents practising family planning, children are generally born in small numbers during a limited time-span and,

TABLE 19. Great Britain. Percentages of couples admitting the use of contraception (inquiry made in 1961)

Social classes	Marriages before 1920	Marriages between 1940 and 1950
I (Professional Business and Non-manual workers)	63·9%	74·4%
II (Skilled manual workers)	62·2%	73·9%
III (Unskilled manual workers)	40·0%	70·6%

obviously, this number is not left to chance since it should correspond exactly to the wishes of the parents. The realization of these plans obviously depends on the efficiency with which couples practise birth control.

If we go by the results of direct inquiries about the use of birth control, then the practice of it seems to be far from general. In the United States, in 1955, Freedman, Whelpton and Campbell only found 70 per cent to be 'motive users' of contraceptive methods; this proportion falls to 52 per cent in rural districts, 69 per cent in small and medium-sized towns, but rises to 74 per cent in large cities. More recently (1961) in Great Britain, Rowntree and Pierce have found percentages ranging from 54 to 73 according to time of marriage; Table 19 gives their findings, by social class.

More striking than the rise in percentage, is the tendency towards uniformity of behaviour. However, the figures given here are probably an understatement of the true situation. In judging the skill with which couples plan their fertility, one must take into account the rate of success in their application of contraception. The information available on this is, however, slight. According to the responses to the investigation led by Freedman, Whelpton and Campbell in the United States[1] 13 per cent of the 2,713 couples questioned had more children than planned, while 66 per cent, although they did not have more than they wanted, were not able to plan the dates of the births as they would have wished. Here too, the difference between the various groups of the population is clear. For instance, if we classify couples by level of education, 7 to 10 per cent of couples who attended high school for at least four years have had more children than planned, while as many as 33 per cent of those who did not go beyond primary education are in the same situation.

Another interesting approach to the subject is through the study of the answers to questions on the number of children desired by a couple. Inquiries in this direction have tried to discover opinions and intentions on various points: couples have been asked about the ideal number of children (in general and in their own milieu), the number of children desired, the number of children expected and so on. The results obtained from such inquiries are all very interesting, but we shall only look at the most striking here.

The sizes of family given in opinion polls are always more restricted than those actually achieved. If only because of the physiological sterility of some couples (between 10 and 20 per cent of marriages concluded in one year can be classed as sterile), childless couples are quite common, although it is exceptional for a childless household to be considered ideal.

[1] *GAF Study*, 1955.

An important point arises from these observations: why is there such a difference between behaviour and opinion? This is something which can only be answered by a general examination of the extent of this difference and the reasons behind it.

It is worth looking closely at the number of children most often mentioned as the size of the ideal family; practically only three figures are ever given: two, three or four children. This mode is interesting in so far as it reflects the norm prevailing in the population in question; a change of mode in the same population is a clear indication of an appreciable modification in the attitude of adults towards the child and its place in the family. It has been noted that, in France, soon after the First World War, the mode changed from two to three children, while, in the United States, the figure has been four for some time, and two in England and Wales. The hierarchy of effective fertility corresponds, then, to the modal dimensions established during the investigations into the size of the ideal family. This seems to invalidate what was said before about a lack of correspondence between opinions and behaviour.

The problem of effective fertility in relation to ideal fertility should be looked at as a whole. If couples behaved in respect of their fertility according to their ideal, they would attempt to reach what they consider to be the correct dimensions without going beyond them. In other words, their fertility would be slightly under the norm they consider ideal, since the sterility of some and the sub-fertility of others would prevent them from reaching the desired dimensions. Calculations made by the present author have shown that the effective total fertility can be reckoned to be between 15 and 20 per cent below the ideal figure. Thus, in a population where the ideal average is three children, the effort to reach this ideal would lead to a final average effective fertility of 2·5

TABLE 20. Total fertility by size of family observed (ideal size)

Population observed	Size of family ideal	actual	Difference	Population observed	Size of family ideal	actual	Difference
Canada 1960	4·31	3·39	−21%	France 1960			
United States 1960	3·63	2·99	−18%	general ideal	2·77	2·38	−14%
Holland 1960	3·28	2·71	−17%	ideal in milieu	2·56	2·21	−14%
United Kingdom 1960	2·78	2·37	−15%	Federal Germany 1958			
France 1956				general ideal	2·59	2·25	−13%
general ideal	2·85	2·44	−14%	ideal under favourable conditions*	2·73	2·26	−17%
ideal in milieu	2·63	2·27	−14%	Hungary	2·27	1·98	−13%

* More precisely: ideal if conditions were very favourable.
SOURCE: R. Pressat, 'The Ideal and the Actual Number of Children', *Studies on Fertility and Social Mobility*, Budapest, 1964.

children. This enables us to construct Table 20 which establishes the correspondence between ideal fertility and effective fertility, always bearing in mind the hypothesis that effective fertility results from the effort to reach ideal fertility.

The last question to be resolved to complete this comparison between behaviour and opinions is how to compare the dimensions reached in the examples given in Table 20 with the final total fertility of the populations under consideration. It will be impossible, however, to go too deeply into methodological detail – this would be beyond the scope of this book. A point which must be made, though, is that the idea of total fertility is a vague one, though all statistical studies show that it depends very much on the age of the woman at the time of marriage. Some idea of the phenomenon can be gained by looking at the figures for France – always remembering, of course, that these are for marriages theoretically not terminated by death or divorce.

Women married before 20 : 3·7 live births
at 20–24 : 2·8 „ „
at 25–29 : 2·2 „ „
at 30–34 : 1·6 „ „
at 35–39 : 0·9 „ „
at 40–49 : 0·2 „ „

Faced with such very variable figures, it is difficult to know which to choose to compare with the results given in Table 20. The problem can be solved by putting the question in this way: what idea of a family pre-exists in the mind of the persons questioned, when asked about the ideal dimensions of a family; in other words, according to what implicit hypothesis have the figures in Table 20 been obtained? It would seem plausible to say that the persons questioned have in mind the usual conditions in which couples come together and start a family: marriage, taking place when the woman is still young and when it is likely to be of some duration.

Based on these considerations, the comparison between declared ideals and actual behaviour shows that, in average terms, what couples consider to be the ideal number of children is almost always *below* their actual number.

This universal difference between ideal and real fertility can depend upon the co-existence of three sub-populations:

(i) one reaching, or at least trying to reach, the desired number of children;

(ii) one going beyond the numbers declared to be desirable;

(iii) one which deliberately remains below the size it considers to be ideal;

the effects of excess fertility in group (ii) outweighing those of sub-fertility in group (iii).

The differences in the division of family size whether ideal or real, seem to justify making these distinctions notwithstanding the difficulties of this kind of comparison.

It is tempting to consider the couples of group (ii) as having failed in their family planning. In reality, the situation is more subtle and implies the existence of sub-groups who went beyond the ideal expressed, either because the latter is not very clear, or does not correspond to their personal views, or because, in certain circumstances, the birth of a child did not seem to interfere with their plans for the future. This vagueness is accentuated by the imperfection of the contraceptive techniques used at the time by the populations observed. These imperfections leave serious possibilities of pregnancy if the latter is not absolutely unwelcome.

With the increasingly widespread use of new and far more effective contraceptives (I.U.D. and the pill), one would imagine that the persons in group (ii) will only have the number of children planned for, in the way group (i) has, using 'classical' contraceptives. If, in the same circumstances, group (iii) did not alter its behaviour (which is not certain, if one interprets the excessive care of this group as being the result of imperfect methods of contraception), then fertility would drop well below the present difference between ideal and real fertility. Taking this difference as the minimum demographic effect of a perfect contraceptive, then it is possible to forecast a drop of 25 per cent in the fertility rate

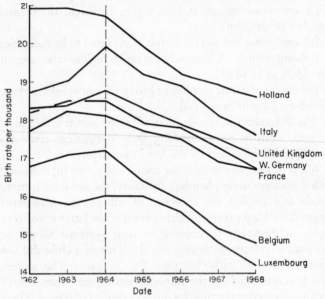

Fig. 11. Recent developments in the birth rates of some western European countries

(this refers to the average number of children born live to each woman and who reach the age of 15). In such conditions, the populations of the West would not be able to ensure their replacement and would be subject to a progressive reduction in the long run.

It remains, however, to decide whether the falling birth rate which affects most western populations is a confirmation of the views expressed above. In the United States and in Canada, the birth rate has dropped in ten years from 25 per cent to about 18 per cent; in France, in England and Wales, West Germany, Italy, Belgium and Holland, one can see a remarkably uniform drop in the birth rate (see Fig. 11). It is, however, really much too early to find the answers to these questions; further, the degree of diffusion of the latest contraceptives, at least in Europe, has not been such as to account for the recent reductions in the fertility rate.

More generally, all judgments and predictions on the situation and the future of demographic phenomena must be extremely cautious. Where population is concerned, there are no immutable laws. What at one time has appeared to be established truth or an inevitable process has been disproved in the following decades, as, for instance, has the belief of thirty years ago in an unavoidable, steep fall in fertility in all categories of the population. In fact, during the last twenty years, western Europe has seen something of a rise in the fertility rate, more marked among the groups who formerly closely limited their fertility rate than among those who had always remained highly fertile. This has led to a greater uniformity of situations and homogeneity of reproductive behaviour.

We have already noted this tendency in the findings from America on fertility by level of education and in the lessening of the difference between rural and urban fertility, there being a greater rise in the latter than in the former.

It is, therefore, undeniable, if one excludes the very slight drop of recent years, and despite the great effectiveness and diffusion of contraceptive techniques, that there has been a certain movement in favour of the family, thus leading to slightly higher fertility than in the recent past. The significance of this change can be examined at the collective level and at the family level.

On the collective, i.e. demographic level, we must consider the repercussions of individual behaviour on demographic evolution. We must also decide what is best for the evolution of the populations of industrialized countries: should there be moderate growth, no growth at all, a slight drop, or a very marked one?

The present level of fertility in western countries shows a moderate annual growth rate; it rarely rises above 1 per cent and is usually around 0·5 per cent. At this rate, populations double in about a hundred years which is in no way disturbing as far as the prospect of over-population in the immediate future goes. A moderate growth of the population has undeniable advantages for countries which enjoy rapid technical change (this point will be discussed in the next chapter), so that the present situation seems to be satisfactory, an assessment which is now more or less universally accepted.

The debate of the ideal size of a family, for the harmonious development of the latter and for the best development of the children's personality, is infinitely more open and can involve very varied preferences and demographic developments.

The matter may be considered from an essentially psychological point of view, although this must involve considerations which are unmistakably favourable to a higher birth rate. A number of authorities who argue from this sort of standpoint claim that the size of the ideal family can vary from three to six children inclusive.[1] The wide gulf separating those who hold such an opinion and those who prefer to have only one child can be clearly seen; and we must not forget the very different demographic consequences which result from these extremes of behaviour.

In fact, very little is known about the relative advantages and disadvantages of small or large families. It has often been

[1] See R. Debré, 'La famille heureuse ou l'optimum familial', *Population* 4, 1950.

observed that the children of large families enjoy less advantageous conditions than the children of smaller families, either as regards I.Q. or the rate of infant mortality. But this could be linked to the size of the family, reducing the resources available per person, rather than to the actual number of children itself. On the other hand, it has been too rapidly concluded that a large family is superior because of the advantages it confers in the moulding of character since it provides prolonged contact with brothers and sisters. It has also been said, quite legitimately, that a large family reduces the possibility of contacts for the child with the adult world, depriving him of the specific advantages which go with this kind of contact. To confirm this theory, it has been observed in certain milieux, with respect to the size of family and socio-economic level, that the results obtained by twins in tests are notably inferior to those obtained by other children.

However, in most modern families, the influence of the size of the family is minimal, since the average size varies very little (three-quarters have between one and four children). It is more legitimate to question the influence of other socio-economic and educational factors and to reach suitable conclusions on that basis.

VIII

ECONOMICS AND POPULATION

THE relationships between population and the level of well-being are numerous and complex. Malthus was one of the first people to consider them from a genuinely vital point of view. Discovering a disparity between the potential growth of a population (growth in geometrical progression) and the growth of the means of subsistence (growth in arithmetical progression), he concluded that poverty would inevitably increase if man did not limit his demographic expansion. These pessimistic views were to be expressed scientifically by David Ricardo and his disciples, in the law of diminishing returns; these economists, though seeing the advantages of demographic expansion at its very beginning, especially when there are still sufficient reserves of land, finally concluded that each additional working unit would lead to a constant reduction in productivity.

These forecasts have been disproved, or, at least, the application of Ricardo's law has been delayed; the great technical progress of the nineteenth and twentieth centuries was to permit an amount of demographic growth which Malthus was unable to envisage. Since the time of Malthus, the population of England has multiplied six times and the population of the world has quadrupled.

Maximum Population, Minimum Population, Optimum Population

Malthus lived at a time when natural demographic conditions were still almost universally prevalent: voluntary limitation of births was still rare and the fight against death still very ineffective. The resulting natural multiplication of the human species found an obstacle in the amount of subsistence available. Briefly, the population tended to reach the maximum level allowed by the technical level of the time. Because of its considerable development, the technical level has consequently allowed the maximum population to rise.

The maximum population has been thus defined: 'the maximum population is badly nourished, of mediocre health, but capable at the same time of producing and sharing equally in production'.[1] However, the existence of a maximum population only corresponds to difficult living conditions such as are never observed by the whole of the human race. The rapid appearance of privileged classes leads to a consumption rate above the strict minimum and thus reduces the maximum population.

In this sphere, the ingenious schemes devised by Sauvy, based on the analyses by Cantillon, show the importance of the social structure of a population and the type of consumption of the privileged classes. Sauvy has put forward the hypothesis of a population of 100 peasants each producing an average of 4,000 vegetable calories a day, of which they can freely dispose of 2,000. The $100 \times 2,000 = 200,000$ calories thus obtained can be used to keep a landowner. He will not consume them directly but will be able, with the help of 90 workmen (servants and artisans) to keep a population at his service. This will require $90 \times 2,000 = 180,000$ calories and 20,000 will remain at his disposal. But if the consumption of natural produce by this landowner, already high, rises – for instance, if this squire keeps dogs or horses or consumes a higher proportion of animal calories (5 or 6 vegetable calories make 1 animal calorie) – he will only be able to keep 80, 70, perhaps 50 workmen. The living population declines from 191

[1] A. Sauvy.

in the first hypothesis to 181, 171, or even 151 in the second. The situation will also change if there is a middle class, the calorie consumption of which will be 5,000 per person; 20 of these persons will consume as much as 50 non-agricultural workers and the populations will be reduced by as much.

If the idea of the existence of a maximum population seems very obvious, the concept of a minimum population is rather less so and the biological factors leading to a minimum level, below which a population is bound to disappear, are as important as the economic factors. First, there is the risk that it will be impossible to conclude marriages among very small populations, because of the limited scope of matrimonial combinations (at least in a monogamic society). There is also the high degree of consanguinity implied in such a situation with a resulting low fertility rate and high death rate.

In fact, the economic arguments in favour of there being a lower level for the population seem to be less imperative in primitive economies, such as those, for instance, which depend upon the simple gathering of food. It is the division of labour, necessary for the various functions permitting certain standards of well-being, which requires the population to remain above a certain level. And, conversely, we can see, in the most developed countries, the appearance of considerable concentrations of humanity to satisfy the greater diversification in the production of goods and services.

The abandonment of a purely basic way of life implies a movement away from minimum size as well as from the maximum in any given territory. The consideration of these extreme limits implies the probable existence of an inter-mediate optimum size.

The search for an optimum is only really justified if there are several objectives in view. Consequently, limitations must be imposed on the realization of each of these objectives in order to obtain the most harmonious results. This means that there is no absolute optimum, but as many optima as there are priorities in the choice of objectives. A population will thus be judged to have reached its optimum level in so far as it provides the maximum well-being for all its members, or the highest possible cultural level, or the greatest expectation of life, or the greatest amount of power for its leaders, etc.

This concept of an optimum, attractive though it is, remains difficult to define if we want to take it as a basis for evaluating the meaning of a desirable population. If an England with 100 inhabitants seems as undesirable as an England with 500 million, it is still more difficult to make a choice between figures ranging from 40 to 80 million, even if agreement can be reached on the identity and priority of the various objectives.

In general, too, questions of maximum, minimum and optimum population usually remain somewhat academic. In particular, the optimum refers to a system of environmental conditions and, consequently, has no absolute value. For instance, should one, in a given country, try to modify the population until it reaches optimum size according to the conditions of the time, or should one modify those conditions to make the actual size of the population optimum? If it could be proved that the optimum population of India was 250 million, it is difficult to see how the first solution could be applicable, since the country already has 500 million inhabitants. The second solution seems more practical, but the fact of a constantly growing population will lead to a permanent race between the production of goods and the size of the population. Finally, there is, of course, no certainty that the optimum will ever be reached.

This last idea should lead us to the study of the influence of the natural growth rate of population on changes in general living conditions; it should also help us to see the connections between demographic data and economic conditions in a dynamic context. The idea of demographic investment enables us to approach this question more closely.

The Cost of Demographic Growth

The high population growth in developing countries is well worth examination, as is the high density of population observed in some of them. Even the most casual observer must somehow feel that this demographic vitality, signified by the extreme youth of the population, is not compatible with a healthy economy, simply because of the human weight which that economy must support. This particular problem can be clarified by quantitative analysis.

The birth of a child means expense for parents and society: food care, education and professional training. Integration into the labour force presupposes the young worker to have access to premises and tools enabling him to produce. In other words, the acceptance of a newcomer by society as a whole implies expenses which it cannot avoid for fear of introducing a less efficient producer, thus reducing the rate of production per person.

In demographically stationary conditions, where births and deaths balance each other, and the population remains constant, the fraction of the wealth of Society assigned annually to the education and integration of young people into the cycle of production does not involve other expense than that of renewal (with possible improvement) of the apparatus of production in its broadest sense (factories, materials, schools, teachers), in short the writing off of the capital employed. The demographic factor appears as a neutral element in this context.

When we come to conditions of growth, we are faced with quite different problems. Let us suppose, for instance, that a population increases by about two per cent every year: the maintenance of the same standards of living in this growing population requires a similar growth of productive capital, growth of the population alone not being enough to produce the supplementary goods needed. The increase in productive capital necessary to cope with demographic growth demands real investments, in addition to those required for the renewal of existing equipment. These investments are called *demographic investments*.

One measures the size of the investments required for an increase in production by introducing the concept of a national rate of interest. A rate of 25 per cent, for example, means that an increase of 100 in the productive capital corresponds to an increase of 25 in annual production. One can also speak of a marginal coefficient of capital, which is 4 in our example: that is to say, in order to achieve an annual increase of 25, the investment needs to be four times greater. The numerical example chosen corresponds more or less to the accepted rate of interest on current investments. A demographic growth rate of 3 per cent, common in developing countries (it can be higher) requires a similar increase in production, that is, an investment to cope with purely demographic factors, four times higher or 12 per cent of the annual production.

A high population growth rate cannot be treated as an isolated feature: there are other characteristics resulting from a high fertility rate, such as the extreme youth of a population and, more generally, an age structure which is economically unfavourable. The economic effects of the population structure are easily quantified by a comparison between the quantities produced and those consumed. Production is related, among other things, to the relative size of the working elements of the population, consumption to general distribution by age, if one accepts the fact of a lower rate of consumption among young and old.

J. Henripin, in his inaugural lecture at the University of Montreal, gives us a very complete picture of the mechanisms we are trying to analyse. He has established that, in terms of units of adult consumption (excess of population over consumption), saving varies from 23·2 per 100 persons when the demographic growth rate is 2·3 per cent to 39·2 when the population is stationary.

TABLE 21

1. Growth rate of the population	2·3%	0·0%
2. Saving possible (a) in units of adult consumption	23·2	39·2
(b) in % of production	21·8%	31·3%
3. Redemption of capital	12%	12%
4. Net investments (2(b) − 3)	9·8%	19·3%
5. Demographic investments*	6·9%	0·0%
6. Economic investments (4–5)	2·9%	19·3%
7. Resultant annual growth of income†	0·7%	4·8%

* with a marginal coefficient of capital equal to 3
† with a marginal coefficient of capital equal to 4
SOURCE: Jacques Henripin, Le coût de la croissance démographique, Les Presses de l'Université de Montréal, Montréal, 1968.

Thus, when there are conditions of demographic growth, the standard of living tends to fall, owing to the need for increased demographic investment, coupled with the diminished possibilities of saving. The combined effect of these two factors is shown in Table 21 which is taken from Henripin's study: the annual increase of income per person varies from 1 to 7, with annual growth rates varying from 2·3 per cent to 0 per cent. Let us not forget that rates above 3 per cent are common in developing countries. This means that the difference in the possibilities of economic growth in the world at present resulting from the difference in demographic growth rates, is even greater than that shown in the table. Deterioration of the standard of living must appear when the annual maximum growth rate of the population of 2·3 per cent given in our table is passed.

Overpopulation

The idea of demographic investment defines the way in which population dynamics can act as a brake on development. This places the emphasis on the difficulties connected with *growth* without taking into account the size of the population. With this point clarified, the demographic difficulties of any black African state of low density appear comparable to those of any island with a very dense population (e.g. Réunion, Mauritius) as long as the natural rates of population growth remain the same. This, of course, amounts to refutation of the idea of overpopulation, at least from the economic point of view.

The idea of overpopulation, corresponding to a static view, can be usefully defined by reference to the idea of optimum population. It can be said that there is overpopulation from the time the optimum figure is passed. This reference to the optimum emphasizes the very varied character of the concept of overpopulation. Is it an obstacle to the realization of the highest standard of living or the attainment of maximum military power, or is it an obstacle to the full employment of the population or even to the concession of maximum social advantages to the inhabitants?

If only implicitly, however, it is to the first of the possible definitions that one refers most frequently when speaking of overpopulation. An excessive number of inhabitants acts as an obstacle to the realization of the highest standards of living compatible with the technical conditions of the age, or, more modestly, in the case of developed countries, it simply makes it impossible to ensure a reasonable standard of living by overcoming the worst privations of the time.

The great uncertainty which surrounds the figures for optimum populations corresponding to precise scales of set objectives, rears its head again when the problem arises of measuring the degree of divergence from these optima and, consequently, of deciding whether there is overpopulation, and on what scale. Similar questions could be asked about a hypothetical underpopulation. However, these uncertainties are of little practical application. Indeed, since considerable possibilities of progress exist everywhere, the recommended course of action is always to stimulate economic development and at the same time attempt to slow down demographic development when the latter competes directly with a rise in productivity.

The Population in Modern Economics

Up to this point my analysis has been concerned with delineating the harmful effects of demographic growth in so far as it works against economic expansion. But has this growth only a negative side?

In fact, we have only tackled certain aspects of the relationship between population and economy. We must now broaden our approach to determine what, in general, are the demographic conditions most capable of sustaining economic growth.

We can say with reasonable certainty that the rapid expansion of population, especially in developing countries, constitutes an obstacle to improving living conditions in those countries. However, the conclusions which can be drawn when we turn to the situation in industrialized countries are less precise. Should the populations of these countries, which usually grow at very moderate rates, try to remain stationary or seek a certain amount of growth?

Clearly, what has been said of the economic cost of demographic growth remains valid, in general, for the populations of advanced economies. In particular, one cannot neglect the fact that these economies, characterized by the volume of the redistribution of income and the high cost of education, the relative importance of the working, and therefore productive age-groups of the population, depend very strictly on the rate of growth of the population and, more precisely, on the rate of fertility which conditions that growth. It has been shown that, with the mortality rate of western countries, a gross reproduction rate of 3 (about 6 live births per woman) only implies that 49 per cent of the population is aged between 15 and 60, whilst a rate slightly over 1, which would cause the population to remain stationary, means 58 per cent are in the same age-groups.

It has also been observed that, in those populations with a high level of employment, the arrival of numerous children presents an obstacle to the economic participation of the woman, while, conversely, such participation is easily possible with a limited family (one or two children).

But this analysis of the advantages of a perfectly stationary population is too one-sided. In fact, this is hardly an optimum situation and a certain demographic dynamism, as long as it remains within moderate limits without creating excessive burdens from growth, presents certain advantages. The most obvious of these advantages lies in the increased rate of renewal of the population; the use of population models shows that, if a population is stationary, the annual contribution in new workers of the working generations can be estimated at 2·3 per cent. This new section of the economically active population exactly replaces the aged, the deceased and the retired. If, however, the population grows at the rate of 1 per cent, the annual contribution of the younger generations to the economically active population becomes almost 3 per cent. In addition, these new elements are much more mobile than their elders who are already engaged in a single activity. During periods of intense economic progress and the subsequent structural modifications in the economy, corresponding modifications in the division of labour must be coped with. One man can cite, for example, the decline of the agricultural population and the expansion of vital industries. All this permits an increased contribution on the part of younger elements of the population who are directed towards expanding occupations, disposing of more skills than would be the case if workers in other specialized occupations were retrained.

Although the stationary population usually includes a greater proportion of persons of active age than a growing population, the total of the active population is older, since, the younger elements, those below 40 years old for example, form a smaller proportion. This increased degree of ageing entails a qualitative depreciation caused by the decline of physical and mental powers with the advancement of age. It is no longer certain that, in respect of their active elements, the populations showing moderate growth are everywhere at a disadvantage in relation to stationary populations.

Still in the sphere of employment, it has been established that a certain amount of demographic growth is a factor conducive to full employment in advanced economies. This is obviously an argument of great weight since this question of full employment is such an important factor in affluent economies. It is an essential element in the well-being of a consumer society because of the possibilities of participation it provides. What comes into operation here is a cumulative process of expansion: a sustained demographic progression increases the demand for goods and services which, in turn, involves investment and then revenue, and this, in its turn, gives a new thrust to investment. This means that a modern economy could not, at present, reconcile itself to demographic inertia.

IV

POPULATION POLICIES

THINKERS were preoccupied with the relationship between population and society long before useful demographic observations could be made. Thus, Confucius in China and Plato in Greece formulated more or less exact laws concerning the evolution or the desirable composition of the population. In his *Laws*, Plato recommends an ideal city of 5,040 citizens, this having the quality of containing a large number of divisors, which would permit the organization of a large number of categories of population sub-groups; each such category would correspond to a division of goods and social work.

Much closer to our own day, the great Moslem thinker Ibn Khaldun (1332–1406), makes the point that a sufficiently dense population makes for better utilization of the workers because of the possibility of specialization of tasks and the greater ease with which political and military security can be assured. Elsewhere, the same author advances the theory of the cyclical fluctuations of population in relation to the fluctuations of the economic, political and social situation.

However, it was during the seventeenth and eighteenth centuries in Europe that a really coherent doctrine, upheld by numerous authors, appeared: mercantilism.

According to the mercantilists the growth of the population presents certain advantages and should be encouraged by the State, though it should be noted that these authors are far more interested in the power of the State than in the well-being of the individual. Therefore, they argue, everything which augments that power must be sought after. An obvious objective is the possibility of increasing returns in manufacture permitted by a large population; this is contrasted with the law of decreasing returns operative in agriculture. It is thus possible, by the indirect action of foreign trade, for the population to be increased to a considerable extent if it is possible to exchange labour for goods; that is, to export manufactured products and to import new materials and foodstuffs.

As a reaction against these populationist views and also against the projects presented by Godwin and Condorcet in the field of social reform, other authors applied themselves to defining the relationship between population and subsistence by emphasizing the effect of the latter on the former. The most famous of these authors, Malthus, was led, as we have seen, to formulate the 'Principle of Population' which provides the first coherent basis for a population policy.

After him, the many discussions, like the increasingly numerous interventions of political power in the field of demography, have always been classified, admittedly a little summarily perhaps, in relation to the attitudes and views of Malthus.

The classical economists of the nineteenth century are to be found on a line leading directly from the thinking of Malthus. From him they take up the argument, developing it with greater subtlety, according to which the growth of population causes a falling off of wages and brings poverty. Contrary, however, to the liberal school of thought at the time, the socialist and Marxist authors deny the existence of a population problem as such and maintain that the fears inspired by demographic expansion will fade away once the defects of the existing social order are corrected.

Instead of carrying out a detailed examination of the currents and shades of thought for which economists, moralists and politicians have been responsible on the subject of population, we shall look at those population policies which have had a practical influence in the life of peoples.

Public authority can act in many directions to affect demographic evolution. In particular, the constituent parts of this evolution, mortality, fertility, and migration, are not immune from the action of governments. This action can show itself, notably, in the protection of public health, the encouragement of the birth rate, family welfare, legislation on abortion and birth control, the control of inland travel and the crossing of national frontiers.

Pro-natalist Policies

Above all, governments have tried to act with measures in favour of an increasing birth rate. The spectre of depopulation is the first to have haunted those responsible for the national interest. In antiquity, the laws of Augustus are the most striking example of the foresight of a great ruler in population matters. Sensing the double threat of corrupted *mores* and the resulting depopulation he promulgated in Rome, then at the height of its splendour, laws facilitating marriage, suppressing adultery and making divorce more difficult. He penalized bachelors and childless couples through changes in the laws of succession; through the *jus trium liberorum*, he granted special privileges in the matter of inheritance and taxation to couples with at least three children.

At the present date, there has been some tendency towards a fear of depopulation in industrialized countries, where the birth rate continued to drop during the second half of the nineteenth century and the first four decades of the twentieth century, on account of economic development and urbanization. France was a rather special case since the decline in the birth rate started in the second half of the eighteenth century:

consequently, movements to encourage fertility were to start there earlier than in other countries.

To encourage a rise in the birth-rate, action can be taken against behaviour which leads towards infertility (suppression of abortion, forbidding of contraceptive propaganda and of the diffusion of contraceptives), or positive measures can be taken to encourage large families (practical aid to families under various forms: allowances, tax-relief, etc.).

In France, the former type of action was taken first. In 1920, after a murderous war, a law strictly forbidding all abortion and publicity for contraception was passed; this law was only abolished in 1968. It is very much open to question whether this law induced a rise in the birth rate or even slowed down the decline which had started 150 years earlier. It is always a delicate matter to rewrite history and one's opinion here will probably depend more on *a priori* ideas on the utility of the law than on an analysis of its effects, which are always difficult to evaluate.

In fact, it was to be the positive measures taken in the early forties, after the passing of the *Code de la Famille*, which undeniably influenced the fertility behaviour of French households. Numerous facts seem to point to a causal relationship between the positive measures taken to increase fertility and its rise. First, there were two changes which happened almost simultaneously. From 1941–1942, newly-married couples behaved noticeably differently from older couples. Furthermore, a close analysis of the various socio-economic categories, each influenced in a different way by the measures in favour of larger families, has shown that the fertility rate rose most among those groups particularly favoured by the new laws. Fig. 12 is very significant in this respect and two facts emerge from it: the rise was sharper among salaried families, who benefited from family allowances, than among independent workers, who received less from the pro-family measures, although the two classes had a similar fertility rate before the war.

This seems to support the idea that public intervention to raise the birth rate can prove effective. Up to that time, in spite of the example of Germany during the Nazi régime, there was considerable doubt whether political action could have any results in this field.

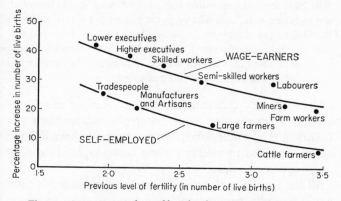

Fig. 12. Average number of live births in France by socio-occupational category of the husband (complete families—wives married before the age of 30)
(SOURCE: Maurice Febvay, 'Niveau et évolution de la fécondité par catégorie socio-professionelle en France', International Congress on Population, Vienna, 1959)

In Germany in 1934, nine months after Hitler's coming to power, and in Austria in 1939, nine months after the *Anschluss*, the birth rate suddenly rose 4 points per 1,000. To begin with, this can only have been the result of the ruthless suppression of abortion by a government which used any means to achieve its ends. But, over a longer period, this high fertility rate must have been the consequence of renewed confidence in a stable government, effective in the fight against unemployment and pronatalist in a number of its policies (for instance, loans were available at the time of marriage).

It was certainly the thought that a fundamental change was necessary which moved the originators of the *Royal Commission on Population*, in Great Britain. The report of the Commission starts with the following statement of policy:

We have deemed it expedient that a Commission should forthwith issue to examine the facts relating to the present population trends in Great Britain; to investigate the causes of these trends and to consider their probable consequences; to consider what measures, if any, should be taken in the national interest to influence the future trend of population and to make recommendations.

The extremely elaborate study undertaken by this Commission, which remains, as a demographic balance sheet of a country, a model of its kind, does not appear to have inspired policies designed to modify current demographic behaviour in any appreciable way.

All the countries claiming to practise orthodox Marxism should logically favour population growth, since socialism, according to its doctrine, should eliminate any barrier to such growth. In fact, the history of demographic policy in the U.S.S.R., and in the other European socialist countries, shows that theory has hardly been followed in practice. The widely proclaimed freedom of the family, and particularly of the woman, in the choice of the number of children, has led the governments of these countries to allow abortion at various times. Alternating with periods of extreme laxity in this matter, there have been others of strict control; until 1936, in the USSR, there had never been any restriction of abortion, but from then on, until around 1955, it was strictly forbidden. Lately, however, a more liberal attitude towards the practice seems to have developed. At the same time, between 1956 and

1958, the popular democracies of Europe introduced a number of extremely permissive measures on abortion, if only to reverse them later, as Rumania did spectacularly in 1967. On the other hand, Albania and East Germany were never part of this movement, because, in the case of the latter, of the grave demographic losses before the building of the Berlin wall. In between these extremes, we find Czechoslovakia and above all Hungary, who, while making legal abortion fairly easy to obtain by women who want it, have had some success with their pro-fertility policies (grants to enable the woman to remain at home while bringing children up, family allowances and other grants). The case of Bulgaria is also interesting, in so far as it testifies to a precise choice by the authorities in the matter of the reproduction of the population: to favour a rising birth rate without encouraging large families. To achieve this, grants and allowances (like leave granted), low for the first child, become appreciably larger for the second and especially the third child, only to become very low again after this.

Finally, the variations and inconsistencies in the policies of the socialist countries show just how hesitant and indecisive the authorities are in making the best possible choice, not only of means but also of ends. On that point the ideas of Marx seem to offer them no help.

Even in the light of recent experience, it is difficult to be definite about what a pro-natalist policy must consist of to be effective. It seems, however, essential to distinguish between those pro-family measures which lead to greater social justice and those which act genuinely in favour of a rising birth rate. Again, certain measures can satisfy both these objectives at the same time. Thus, since the standard of living diminishes most in a household at the birth of the second or third child (the wife is often incapable of undertaking work, accommodation becomes too small, and so on), any action intended to compensate for the fall in income will have a pro-natalist effect. But a truly pro-natalist point of view should urge that families should not be helped until they have produced two or three children, since the first child usually comes because of the spontaneous wish of couples, without any material inducement being necessary. In this case, the concern for social justice and the attempt at pro-natalist action lead to the adoption of conflicting solutions. Conditions for the granting of child allowances (the allowance is made, for example, only if the birth comes less than two years after the marriage or the preceding birth) satisfy an exclusively pro-natalist objective.

In fact, it seems that the majority of industrialized nations which have developed a system of family welfare, have done so much more often with a social end in mind than with the intention of modifying the direction or rhythm of demographic evolution. The pro-natalist aims of family policy are most striking in fundamentally Malthusian countries, whether this Malthusianism be long-standing (as in France), or of recent origin (as in some socialist countries, where it is very marked).

Anti-natalist policies

In many parts of the Third World, thought on the subject has hardly started to evolve and fertility is still what it always has been, that is, very near the natural level, every woman having an average of 5 to 8 children. At the same time, therapeutic techniques from abroad, cheap and easy to distribute, have led to a fall in the death rate. The result is an imbalance between mortality and birth rate, which has meant a growth rate which nineteenth century Europe never knew, even at the peak of its demographic expansion. A prospective doubling of the population every 25 years is a common occurrence in developing countries.

In such circumstances it was unavoidable that governments should try to slow down a birth rate which did not appear likely to decline of its own accord. However, it was another country, Japan, which took the first official measures to diminish demographic expansion.

Having been totally engaged in military effort, and deeply affected by the destruction caused by bombing, Japan found herself, in 1946, with her industrial production reduced to 31 per cent of the 1934–36 level. War losses amounted to more than two million human lives. The pre-war standard of living was to be reached again only in 1950.

The reunion of members of families who had been separated for a long time (most frequently since 1937; as early as 1938 these separations had had an effect on the birth rate) and the increased possibility of marriage with the return of peace caused the birth rate to rise appreciably:

> 1947: 34·3 births per 1,000 inhabitants;
> 1948: 33·5 births per 1,000 inhabitants;
> 1949: 33·0 births per 1,000 inhabitants.

Death rates dropped shortly, as they did in all countries as new therapeutic methods became more widespread after the war. Lastly, the huge numbers of returning Japanese, who had been established in formerly occupied territories, meant an influx of five million people in five years. Altogether, by natural growth and immigration, eleven million people were added to the population between November 1945 and October 1950.

It was in this demo-economic context (a ruined country, a rapidly growing population – 83 million inhabitants in 1950 – and consequently, with public opinion very sensitive to questions of population) that the Eugenics Law of July 1948 was passed.

No serious moral or religious obstacle stood in the way of the diffusion of a national policy of birth restriction in a

country which had a certain tradition of abortion and infanti-
cide. In particular, the two principal religions, Buddhism and
Shintoism, are not fundamentally opposed to either abortion
or contraception. Western religions, even Roman Catholicism,
have had too little influence for their opposition to have
counted for anything. In fact, Catholic opposition showed
itself by way of the Catholic personnel at the American military headquarters which, for that reason, delayed the pro-
motion of birth control which was favoured by the senior
authorities of the Occupation.

Again, the very definite distinction which has become
established in the West between contraception (prevention of
conception) and abortion (destruction of the foetus and therefore of a living being) does not exist in Japan where the
dividing line is established only at birth.

It must be remembered, too, that the military and strategic
arguments in support of a populationist policy had dis-
appeared in the defeated and considerably weakened Japan of
the years 1945–50.

There was, then, a whole collection of conditions which
came together to encourage the population to reduce its
birth rate considerably, without any obstacle other than
practical ones affecting the choice of methods. If, among these,
the one which least disgusts our Western mentality, contraception, has played until now only a minor part, it has
nevertheless been anticipated in the eugenics law as one of the
essential methods of reducing fertility.

But it is the practice of abortion which was to lead, at least
at the beginning, to a decline in the fertility rate: in ten years,
births fell by 40 per cent, but at the cost of more than one
million abortions a year (compared to 1·6 million live births).
In spite of a considerable information campaign and the
availability to the public of all known contraceptive means,
the demographic effect of contraception is still relatively small.

It is remarkable that, with the spread of these practices and after possible failures, couples practising contraception still favour the easiest means: today three quarters of those who practice contraception use means (abstention, condom), which are available in countries adverse to the distribution of contraceptive devices, such as France. 43 per cent of couples practise contraception permanently (40 per cent in the country, 47 per cent in the cities), but 63 per cent are aware of it, having practised it at some time in their lives. Inquiries show that very few couples disapprove of contraception.

Public opinion, then, is not unfavourable and abortion is merely an easy way out; it seems that the unpleasantness of such an operation ultimately encourages women to practise contraception, while in the case of those practising contraception regularly abortion will only occur in the event of a failure of contraception.

It is thus justifiable to believe that contraception is progressing in Japan. It is significant, however, that 15 to 20 million abortions were necessary at first to reduce the birth rate to a satisfactory level.

A clearer realization of the obstacles to development involved in a demographic explosion in the Third World has led a growing number of countries to favour a policy of family planning. This collective sensitiveness to the grave problems of uncontrolled fertility is expressed in the declaration by the Secretary-General of the United Nations on 10 December 1966, Rights of Man day. This declaration was signed by the heads of state of twelve countries. It reads as follows

We believe that the population problem must be recognized as a principal element in long-range national planning if governments are to achieve their economic goals and fulfil the aspirations of their people.

We believe that the great majority of parents desire to have the knowledge and means to plan their families; that the opportunity to decide the number and spacing of children is a basic human right.

We believe that lasting and meaningful peace will depend to a considerable measure upon how the challenge of population growth is met.

We believe the objective of family planning is the enrichment of human life, not its restriction; that family planning, by assuring greater opportunity to each person, frees man to attain his individual dignity and reach his full potential.

Recognizing that family planning is in the vital interest of both the nation and the family, we, the undersigned, earnestly hope that leaders around the world share our views, and join with us in this great challenge for the well-being and happiness of people everywhere.

At the same time, 27 governments of developing countries have issued declarations, taken decisions, applied policies indicating their agreement with the need to encourage family planning.

If, in this movement, the role of the U.S.S.R. has been discreet, it should nevertheless be stressed that the attitude of this country has changed considerably. It is a long time since the Ukrainian delegate declared at the United Nations:

'We do not accept that, in this place, anyone should suggest the limitation of marriages or births in marriage. Any such proposition must be considered barbaric'.

Indeed, the worrying aspect of present-day demographic growth in developing countries has gradually become clear to everybody, even to the most generously utopian minds. The fact that this situation is new is even more worrying (as was said before, never in their history have the industrial countries known such a demographic explosion). The findings of economists, echoed by demographers, have shown that the resultant demographic investments entailed by an uncontrolled birth rate are an obstacle to any development.

At the same time, more efficient means of limitation of

births have become available, considerably altering the demographic problems of developing countries. Up to the beginning of the nineteen-sixties, only means involving great care and persistence in application were available. They were used only by strongly motivated populations, whose cultural development was sufficiently advanced. With the introduction of oral contraceptives and of the I.U.D., the technical aspect of contraception has been much simplified and great hopes are based on the diffusion of such means and particularly of the second.

It remains true that the effort of diffusion necessary must be gigantic for the demographic effects of modern methods of contraception to be felt. Since they often only reach women who have already had several children, publicity campaigns for the insertion of the I.U.D. only have a marginal influence on the number of births, and the same applies to such measures as sterilization or efforts to raise the age of marriage.

In fact, the main developing countries where the birth rate has dropped noticeably are Puerto Rico and a few isolated territories in Asia with Chinese populations: Formosa, Hong Kong, Singapore. It should be mentioned too, that these countries have a particularly low infant mortality rate, since less than 25 children under 1 year die per 1,000 births (a rate comparable to that of advanced European countries).

Thus, it is not impossible that circumstances favourable to reduction of infant mortality could also lead to a fall in the birth rate: this is especially likely when there is a general attitude of foresight, which implies more responsible procreation as well as better care for the child. The child usually becomes more important and frequent births become less desirable. Finally, the political element in the change in fertility behaviour among these populations appears to have had only a nebulous influence and the contribution of the new contraceptive techniques would seem to be negligible.

Other Aspects

In the present combination of circumstances, there is a tendency to remember most clearly those population policies intended to modify the birth rate in one way or other. However, all the other demographic phenomena are affected by governmental intervention.

As far as mortality is concerned, all societies attach great value to the maintenance of human life, the fight against illness and the attainment of the longest life possible. At certain times in their history, however, some governments have rejected the priorities implied by the pursuit of the longest life for the largest number, either because of an aggressive war or racialist policy or because of the need to oppose other warlike and racialist governments: the terrible hecatombs of the last war bear witness to this.

In time of peace, public health is gradually becoming a priority concern in all countries. Protection of health and life starts with the prevention of disease and accidents among the more vulnerable categories of the population: young children, workers, pregnant women and old people. Ultimately, it is the whole policy of social welfare which makes itself felt in this field: housing, redistribution of income, social security, education and the struggle against various social ills. The increasing intervention of the State is clearly responsible for the rapid spread of medical progress and hygiene. Lastly, without appearing to be a conscious element of population policy, the constant and widespread action of governments in public health and social matters has probably had more influence than anything else on demographic evolution.

The migrations which change the geographical distribution of population are often politically inspired. This is a universal fact as far as international migrations are concerned and it is often the case in movements between different parts of the same state. At the present time, large movements of population have become indispensable when the coexistence of different ethnic and cultural groups proves impossible: Moslems and Hindus in India, Moslems and Europeans in North Africa, national minorities in central Europe and the Balkans, especially after changes in frontiers. The cost of such population movements has always been high in money as well as in the suffering incurred by the displaced. The decisions taken in this sphere are usually the result of unbearable situations which can only be solved by the complete separation of the incompatible communities.

Labour migration is less unpleasant and is necessary in the modern economy because of the diversification of work and the abandonment of the more thankless jobs by the nationals of the developed countries. The State is rather an intermediary than an initiating force in this case, which really originates in economic necessity.

More generally, it could be said that political action in this sphere should aim as much at lessening the difficulties of transplantation, by organizing the best reception possible, as at intervening in decisions to move individuals.

APPENDIX

DEMOGRAPHIC ANALYSIS

THE knowledge of a certain language, of certain methods of description and of certain analytical principles is needed for anything more than a purely superficial examination of the problems of population. The following introduction to the techniques of demography, however, only deals with very simple concepts which should not worry the uninstructed reader.

The demographer describes demographic phenomena (mortality, nuptiality, fertility) within a formal framework; he calculates specific indices (rates, quotients) and is thus led to a consideration and analysis of population structures. I want, now, to consider these three types of question.

The Tables and Diagrams of Demographic Analysis

John Graunt is, as we have seen, the great initiator of the *life table*. In the form in which it was originally conceived, a life table makes it possible to show precisely how the members of a generation progressively disappear. For instance, the information in Table 22 gives us certain elements of this description for the 1820 generation of Frenchwomen: column l_x gives the survivors at different birthdays (0, 1 year, 2 years. . . 100 years). Column d_x gives the deaths between two successive birthdays; thus

$$d_x = l_x - l_{x+1}$$

and:

$$d_4 = l_4 - l_5$$
$$= 74,607 - 73,167 = 1,440$$

and finally q_x, the annual mortality quotient, is defined by the formula

$$q_x = \frac{d_x}{l_x}$$

This is, then, the proportion of persons alive, at a given

TABLE 22. Life table for the 1820 generation
of Frenchwomen (extracts)

Age	x	l_x	d_x	q_x (per 1,000)
0 year		100,000	15,270	152·7
1 year		84,730	5,253	62·0
2 years		79,477	2,941	37·0
3 years		76,536	1,929	25·2
4 years		74,607	1,440	19·3
5 years		73,167	1,096	15·0
50 years		47,016	649	13·8
80 years		10,336	1,447	140
100 years		20		

SOURCE: P. Delaporte, 'Evolution de la mortalité en Europe depuis les origines de l'état civil', *Statistique Générale de la France, Etudes démographiques* No 2.

birthday, who die before the next birthday. It can easily be established that

$$d_x = l_x q_x \text{ and } l_{x+1} = l_x(1 - q_x)$$

The three series $\{l_x\}$, $\{d_x\}$, $\{q_x\}$ provide the basis for Fig. 13.

It can be seen that the risk of death is at a minimum around the twelfth year and that after that age the risks increase steadily, the limit to human longevity being somewhere around 100 years.

Starting from a life table a very significant concept can be calculated: average life or expectation of life at birth, which is, in fact, the average age of the deceased in the table. This

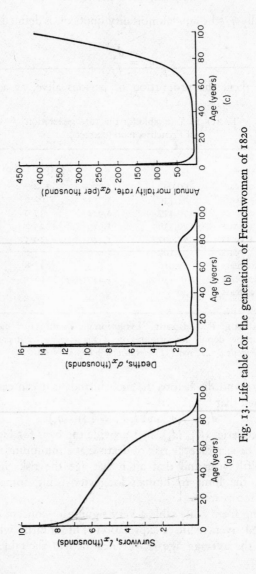

Fig. 13. Life table for the generation of Frenchwomen of 1820

expectation of life at birth is denoted by e_0 and it can thus be easily established that

$$e_0 = 0 \cdot 5 + \frac{l_1 + l_2 + l_3 + \ldots}{l_0}$$

The complete data of the French table in question give the following result: $e_0 = 41 \cdot 0$ years.

TABLE 23. Abridged life table for the female generation of England and Wales born in 1876.

x	l_x	d_x	$5^q{}_x{}^*$		l_x	d_x	$5^q{}_x$
0	1,000,000	131,964	131·96	65	487,761	64,314	131·86
1	868,036	99,519	114·65	70	423,447	86,493	204·26
5	768,517	21,549	28·04	75	336,954	106,283	315·42
10	746,968	10,862	14·54	80	230,671	103,906	450·45
15	736,106	14,470	19·66	85	126,765	79,030	623·44
20	721,636	14,788	20·49	90	47,735	38,190	800·05
25	706,848	15,847	22·42	95	9,545	8,867	928·92
30	691,001	17,319	25·06	100	678		
35	673,682	19,290	28·63				
40	654,392	22,125	33·81	* Except for $x = 0$ and $x = 1$;			
45	632,267	23,090	36·53	it is thus a question of 1^q0			
50	609,168	29,872	49·04	and 4^q1; these quotients are			
55	579,296	38,161	65·87	expressed as per 1,000. SOURCE:			
60	541,135	53,374	98·63	*The Chester Beatty Research Institute Serial Abridged Life Tables*, London, 1962.			

Table 23 is an example of an abridged table, the data concerning certain birthdays only (1 year and multiples of five; the quotients considered are thus quinquennial quotients measuring death risks at intervals of five years). One can also calculate an average expectation of life at birth, which, in this case, comes to 50·9 years.

Thus presented, the life table is the statistical history of a generation in respect of mortality; it is a piece of historical description which takes us back into the fairly distant past, since a generation life table can only be constructed after that generation has become extinct, that is, about 100 years after its birth.

TABLE 24. Life tables for England and Wales (1963–65)

Males				Females		
l_x	d_x	$5^q x$ (per 1,000)	Age x	l_x	d_x	$5^q x$ (per 1,000)
10,000	259	259·0	0	10,000	204	204·0
9,741	24	24·6	5	9,796	16	16·3
9,717	19	19·6	10	9,780	12	12·3
9,698	47	48·5	15	9,768	19	19·5
9,651	52	53·9	20	9,749	22	22·6
9,599	47	49·0	25	9,727	29	29·8
9,552	57	59·7	30	9,698	40	41·2
9,495	86	90·6	35	9,658	64	66·3
9,409	143	152·0	40	9,594	105	109·4
9,266	242	261·2	45	9,489	164	172,8
9,024	412	456·6	50	9,325	241	258·4
8,612	680	789·6	55	9,084	360	396·3
7,932	1,038	1,309	60	8,724	556	637·3
6,894	1,366	1,981	65	8,168	850	1,041
5,528	1,589	2,875	70	7,318	1,266	1,730
3,939	1,611	4,090	75	6,052	1,682	2,779
2,328	1,304	5,601	80	4,370	1,908	4,366
1,024			85	2,462		

There are other life tables which work on quite different principles and whose function is to facilitate the continuing observation of mortality from one civil year to another: these are the *short-term or current life tables*.

In any population in a given year, about 100 generations coexist; during that year each generation runs a certain risk of death; one can thus measure for one generation (the youngest) the risk between 0 and 1 year, then for the following generation, the risk between 1 and 2 years and so on. Technically speaking, each generation makes it possible to determine an annual quotient of mortality, the hundred generations giving the series $q_0, q_1, q_2, \ldots q_{100}$. If one submits an *imaginary generation* of 10,000 newly-born to the conditions of mortality

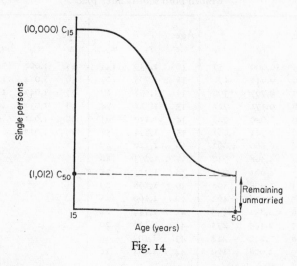

Fig. 14

defined by these quotients, the resultant life table sums up *the conditions of mortality for the year*. This is how the life tables in Table 24 have been constructed for England and Wales in 1963–65; and it is thus, and *only thus*, that one can establish for a given civil year the average length of life or expectation of life at birth, which sums up the mortality conditions for the year. In our example, the averages are, respectively, 86·3 years for men and 74·4 years for women, thus emphasizing male excess mortality (on average, men live six years less than women) which is a nearly universal phenomenon.

The *nuptiality table* is identical in its form to the life table; it describes how single persons of a given sex in a given generation marry. It is thus possible to follow the generation from the minimal age of marriage (in many countries, 15 years for women, 18 for men) to the age when the number of marriages

TABLE 25. Nuptiality table for the generation of French-women born shortly after 1900

Age x	c_x	m_x	Age x	c_x	m_x	Age x	c_x	m_x
15	10,000	57	30	1,839	134	45	1,068	14
16	9,943	176	31	1,705	107	46	1,054	12
17	9,767	396	32	1,598	87	47	1,042	11
18	9,371	722	33	1,511	74	48	1,031	10
19	8,649	928	34	1,437	63	49	1,021	9
20	7,721	1,061	35	1,374	54	50	1,012	
21	6,660	1,062	36	1,320	47			
22	5,598	937	37	1,273	40			
23	4,661	753	38	1,233	35			
24	3,908	594	39	1,198	29			
25	3,314	462	40	1,169	25			
26	2,852	355	41	1,144	22			
27	2,497	275	42	1,122	20			
28	2,222	214	43	1,102	18			
29	2,008	169	44	1,084	16			

taking place can be considered negligible (50 years is normally considered as the upper limit). Furthermore this table is calculated on the assumption that there is no mortality, which poses certain theoretical and technical problems. The assumption of no mortality is of the greatest importance in that it permits us to make pure and unequivocal measurements of the phenomenon. Fig. 14 is illustrated by the nuptiality table given in Table 25. It gives the series for single persons $\{c_x\}$ and omits the series for marriages $\{m_x\}$.

From this it is easy to establish that

$$m_x = c_x - c_{x+1}$$

The existence of permanent spinsters (the 1,012 remaining spinsters at the age of 50) means that

$$\frac{1012}{10,000} = 10 \cdot 12\%$$

of the women of that generation have never married and that consequently

$$1 - 10 \cdot 12\% = 89 \cdot 88\%$$

have concluded a first marriage. This last relationship defines

TABLE 26. Percentages of single persons at different ages

Country	Year	Males			Females		
		20–24 years	25–29 years	45–49 years	20–24 years	25–29 years	45–49 years
England and Wales	1951	76	35	10	52	22	15
United States	1950	59	24	9	32	13	8
France	1954	82	38	11	57	23	10
Ireland	1951	95	77	32	82	54	26
Sweden	1950	84	49	16	60	26	18

the *intensity* of nuptiality among unmarried women in the generation in question. Here we have a new concept which could not exist in the case of mortality for the very obvious reason that all humans are mortal and the total probability of death is always 100 per cent. From the series of marriages one can calculate the average age at first marriage which more or less sums up the rate at which marriages are concluded.

If the calculations of a table of nuptiality are rather complex, the determination of certain elements of these tables is particularly easy in certain circumstances: for instance, when one knows the distribution of the population according to sex, age and marital status, as is usually possible from censuses. Table 26 gives the data for the years around 1950 obtained from that source: the percentages of single persons thus obtained have more or less the same significance as the single persons c_x in a nuptiality table. It may be seen that the percentage at 45–47

TABLE 27. Table of general fertility for France and table of legitimate fertility for Great Britain

France			Great Britain		
woman's age (years) x	n_x	D_x	duration of marriage (years) x	n_x	D_x
15	4	0	0	349	0
16	10	4	1	366	349
17	23	14	2	375	715
18	43	37	3	271	1,030
19	66	80	4	250	1,301
20	92	146	5	225	1,551
25	146	784	10	115	2,476
30	97	1,425	15	63	3,049
35	54	1,821	20	22	3,364
40	21	2,022	25		3,466
45	4	2,087	36		3,479
48		2,094			

France: Generations born just after 1900.

Great Britain: First marriages concluded in 1900–1909 – wife under 45 years of age at marriage.

SOURCE: *The Trend and Pattern of Fertility in Great Britain. A Report on the Family Census of 1946*, by D. V. Glass and E. Grebenik.

years varies considerably; it is particularly high in Ireland (32 and 26 per cent implying total probabilities of nuptiality of the order of 68 per cent for men and 74 per cent for women). Percentages in the same country can differ according to sex; this results from a greater or lesser imbalance between men and women of marriageable age: in countries of emigration such as England and Wales where there is a deficit of men (since they are more likely to emigrate) nuptiality is more intense among them (they marry more easily, being in a minority) than it is among the women.

In the same way as one constructs short-term life tables, one can construct short-term nuptiality tables. However, for different reasons, the results thus obtained are very difficult to interpret, the problems of determining nuptiality conditions of a given period, of a given year for instance, being still unsolved.

Fertility tables are usually somewhat different from those for mortality or nuptiality; this is especially because one most frequently considers all births to a woman, without regard to birth order. It is, however, possible to construct fertility tables for one generation (birth cohort) or for a cohort of marriages.

One example of each list is given in Table 27. In one case the basis is the fifteenth birthday and in the other the initiation of marriage; by accumulating the number of births, one arrives at the total fertility, in both cases, by duration x

$$D_x = n_{15} + n_{16} + \ldots + n_{x-1}$$

The total fertility is reached when all the children are born (at 48 years of age or after 36 years of marriage); that is respectively

2,094 live births per 1,000 women

3,479   "   "   " 1,000 marriages

2,094 and 3,479 can also be considered as measurements of the intensity of the phenomenon (respectively general fertility and legitimate fertility), and the distribution of births according to age of the woman or the duration of the marriage allows us to calculate an average age or an average duration of marriage at the time of the birth of the children.

It should perhaps be added that it is possible, in principle, to construct fertility tables for a limited time-span, in a similar fashion to those for nuptiality; but these will be as uncertain in their interpretation as the nuptiality tables.

The Rates

The varieties of table described above are descriptive models based on certain types of quantitative analysis in demography. The presentation of information in this form is usually preceded by the calculation of extremely elementary indices, among which are the rates. We shall quickly examine the significance of those most frequently used.

The crude rates are the relationships of the marriages, births and deaths of one year to the average population of that year. For instance, the average population of England and Wales in 1967 (population around the middle of the year) has been estimated at 48,390,800 and during that year there were:

386,052 marriages
832,164 births
542,516 deaths

The result of this is a *crude marriage rate* of

$$\frac{386,052}{48,390,800} = 8 \cdot 0 \text{ per 1,000 inhabitants}$$

or of 16·0 per 1,000 if one considers the persons married instead of the marriages (the figure is twice the preceding one). It also gives a *crude birth rate* of

$$\frac{832,164}{48,390,800} = 17 \cdot 2 \text{ per 1,000 inhabitants.}$$

And finally, it gives a *crude death rate* of

$$\frac{542,516}{48,390,800} = 11 \cdot 2 \text{ per 1,000 inhabitants}$$

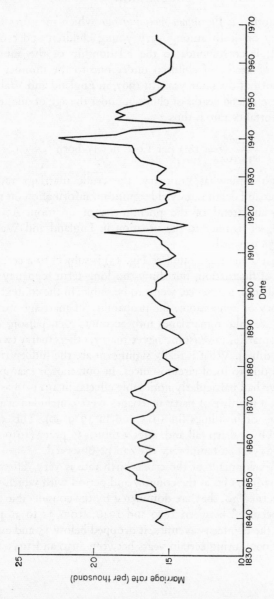

Fig. 15. Crude marriage rates in England and Wales, 1837–1967

Worth noting is the *infant mortality rate* which measures the frequency of death among very young children under one year old; it corresponds to the relationship of the annual number of deaths of children under one to the number of newly-born of the same year. In 1967, in England and Wales, there were 15,266 deaths of children under the age of one; the infant mortality rate is thus

$$\frac{15,266}{832,164} = 18\cdot3 \text{ per 1,000 newly-born}$$

Though somewhat summary, the crude marriage rates, birth rates and death rates yield significant information on the situation and trend of the phenomena in question. As an example, let us refer to the situation in England and Wales from 1838 onwards.

The crude marriage rate (see Fig. 15) is subject to a certain amount of fluctuation, but shows no long-term tendency to rise or fall and, in essence, seems to be stable. In the context of the history of generations, the probability of marriage varies little. If we take remarriages into account, each person, on average, marries once (some never marry, others marry twice or three times). What is really significant are the sudden rises and falls due to local circumstances. In our chosen example, wars have had particularly noticeable effects: in 1914–18 as in 1939–45, a number of hasty marriages were concluded at the beginning of hostilities (in 1915 and in 1939–40). This was followed by a sharp fall and, after a return to peace (1919–20 and in 1945–48) a temporary rise can be observed.

The development of the crude birth rate is very different (see Fig. 16). As far as the country and period with which we are concerned go, they are dominated by the considerable fall which occurred between 1880 and 1940: from 35 to 36 per 1,000 in the eighteen-seventies, it dropped below 15 and even 14 per 1,000 during certain years between 1930 and 1945. At

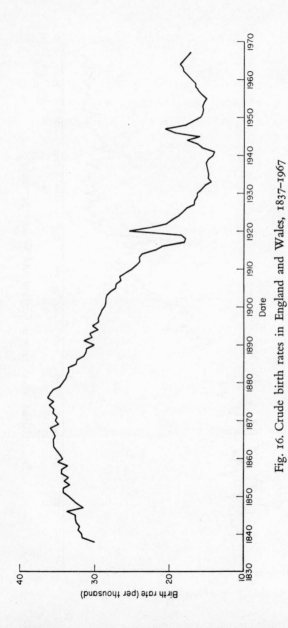

Fig. 16. Crude birth rates in England and Wales, 1837–1967

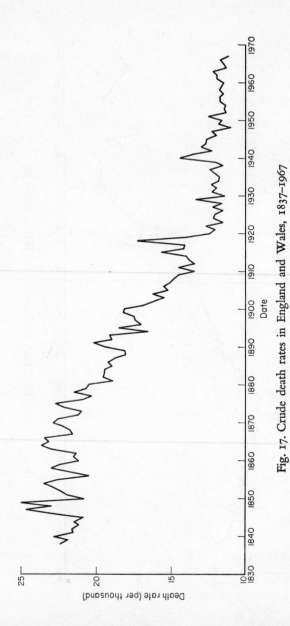

Fig. 17. Crude death rates in England and Wales, 1837–1967

the same time, considerable fluctuations still occur due to war (a drop during the actual conflict, followed by an appreciable rise). The effects of the economic depression in the thirties should be emphasized: the birth rate dropped to its lowest level, apart from the very low level of the war years which followed. One should note, too, the rise in recent years (after 1955), the result of a rise in total fertility of successive generations and of a fall in the age at maternity (women marry younger and have their children earlier in marriage).

The curve of the crude death rate (see Fig. 17) differs from the other two. Compared with the birth rate, a smaller decline within a shorter period is noticeable. This occurs between 1875 and 1920 and shows itself in a drop from 22 to 12 per 1,000. The fluctuations from one year to the next are sharper than in the case of the birth rate. This is particularly true for the years before 1875, when the influence of epidemiological conditions was even more evident than now. Incidentally, the rise in 1918 due to Spanish influenza is well worth noting (the rise during the war period is not due to military losses which are not included in the calculation of the rate given in this figure). The relative stagnation since 1920 appears to contradict the appreciable increase since that date in the expectation of life at birth (the gain is about fifteen years). But it must be realized that the ageing of the population, which is on the increase, would itself, all other things being equal, tend to produce a rise of the crude death rate. That this rise has not occurred in reality is because the increase in the average length of life has almost exactly counterbalanced the effects of the ageing process.

The need for a more precise idea of these phenomena has led to the calculation of the rates for specific age-groups: ten-year groups, five-year groups, and even single years. This is how the infant mortality rate, which measures the frequency of death during the first year of life, was calculated. There is little more to add on these age-specific rates (which can be applied in various ways, such as the fertility rate by duration of marriage) except that they are closely related either to the quotients of the tables (the mortality quotient q_x of Table 23 for example) or to the events (marriages m_x of Table 25, births n_x of Table 27) of the tables of nuptiality and fertility. One of the principal reasons for calculating the rates by age or period is simply to have a means of drawing up suitable tables.

Population Structures

The demographer must not only concern himself with demographic events (marriages, births, deaths) but also with the demographic conditions which these events bring about.

At a given time, a population is characterized by its total number and by the way the components of this total number are distributed by such characteristics as sex, age, marital condition, economic activity, educational level, length of schooling, number of live-births to the females. A large part of demographic analysis is devoted to the interrelation of such structures, which do not arise solely from consideration of demographic characteristics.

In analysing the structure of a population, the aim is to get a better picture of the nature of population; and also to perceive the movements likely to affect the existing structure. These general ideas can be illustrated by a single example – the composition of the population of Great Britain by marital status at the 1966 census. We shall only consider the classification of the population by sex and age, following the division into single and married persons (including among the latter widowed and divorced persons). This gives us the following proportion of single persons (per cent).

One usually notices a drop in proportions of single persons with advancing age; this tendency is normal and results from

Age	Males	Females	Age	Males	Females
20	88·2	65·3	45	9·6	8·7
			46	9·4	8·6
25	35·7	18·4	47	9·8	9·2
			48	9·4	9·4
30	17·1	9·8	49	9·3	9·8
31	15·5	9·5			
32	14·7	8·8	50	8·9	9·8
33	14·0	9·0	51	8·9	9·8
34	13·6	8·7	52	8·1	10·0
			53	8·7	10·5
35	13·2	8·8	54	8·7	10·7
36	12·7	8·8			
37	12·4	8·6	55	8·6	11·2
38	12·4	8·4	56	8·2	11·8
39	11·9	8·9	57	8·3	12·1
			58	7·9	12·6
40	11·6	8·5	59	8·2	13·0
41	11·0	8·9			
42	11·1	8·9			
43	10·3	8·8			
44	10·0	8·5			

what is called the age effect. But it can also be seen that the situation may rapidly become less clear-cut, especially among women, where the proportions may even increase with age. This is called the *generation effect;* the proportion observed in one generation, at a given age, can be higher than that reached by the immediately preceding generation of one year earlier. Since it is unlikely that two generations would have similar histories, the generation effect is always present, but it only becomes obvious as the proportions of single persons increases with age and this would not happen if only the age effect were operating. In the present instance, the generation effect tends to earlier marriages and to a higher probability of marriage.

Reproduction

Basically a population is in a continuous state of renewal: new elements continually join it (by birth or immigration) and other elements leave it (by death or emigration). The numerical evolution of a population is governed by this process of entry and exit and also by the duration of the stay within the population.

TABLE 28. Net reproduction rates (R_0) of the generations of Frenchwomen born shortly after 1900.

Age x years	Births given in Table 27 (per 1,000 women)	Probability of survival from birth to age $(x+0.5)$	Effective births
15	4	0·7787	3
16	10	0·7757	8
17	23	0·7724	18
18	43	0·7688	33
30	97	0·7217	70
31	88	0·7182	63
32	79	0·7149	56
45	4	0·6703	3
46	2	0·6669	·1
47	1	0·6636	1
		Total	1,534

Births of girls: $\dfrac{1,534}{1,000} \times 0.488 = 0.749 = R_0$

A rough idea of the quantitative aspect of this process can be obtained by calculating the annual growth rate which, in the case of a closed population (one with no emigration or immigration) is called the rate of natural increase. This rate is the relationship of the surplus of births over deaths to the average population; in 1967 in England and Wales, this was

$$\frac{832,164 - 542,516}{48,390,800} = 6.0 \text{ per 1,000 inhabitants}$$

Obviously, this is also the difference between the birth rate and the death rate,

$$17 \cdot 2 - 11 \cdot 2 \text{ per } 1,000$$

To obtain more precise information on the renewal of the population, the *net rate of reproduction* (R_0) is calculated. This is, in fact, the number of females born live to each female of a given generation. Thus, the girls born in France around 1900 will have daughters; by calculating the relationship of the number of the latter to that of the former, the net reproduction rate is obtained. It is interesting to note that such a rate is the result of combining a general fertility table and a life table, as shown in Table 28. It is possible to calculate a net rate of female reproduction and a net rate of male reproduction which are not generally equal. It is usual, however, to refer only to the female rate.

A net rate of reproduction below 1 means that at birth the generation concerned does not wholly replace itself, while a rate above 1 indicates an increase in the size of generations from mother to daughter. If the net reproduction rate were to continue unchanged, this would lead, in the long run, to a decrease of population in the first case and to an increase in the second case, while a stationary condition would result from the intermediate situation $(R_0 = 1)$.

SELECT BIBLIOGRAPHY

THERE is no work which covers the whole field of demography satisfactorily, which is hardly surprising, given its dimensions. Consequently, the emphasis in this bibliographical guide will be on the statistical, the sociological, the historical or the economic aspects of population study, according to the author.

However, there are a few comprehensive works of general interest, which should be mentioned: *The Study of Population*, ed. Philip M. Hauser and Otis D. Duncan, University of Chicago Press, 1959. In this work the authors try to define demography as a science; they consider the progress of research in various countries and the principal results; they describe the connections with related disciplines (ecology, genetics, geography and so on).

With fewer claims to be exhaustive, the reports of symposia give very full accounts of certain aspects of demography. The following should be noted: *Demographic and Economic Change in Developed Countries*, Princeton University Press, 1960. This is devoted to fertility problems in developed countries and to the connections between economy and population.

Public Health and Population Change, ed. Mindel C. Sheps and Jeanne Clare Ridley, University of Pittsburgh Press, 1965. This work covers a wider field, examining problems of historical demography, family planning, degree of fertility and contraception.

Much more specific, as its title indicates, is *Research in Family Planning*, ed. Clyde V. Kiser, Princeton University Press, 1962; also *Family Planning and Population Programmes*, ed. B. Berelson *et al.*, Chicago, 1966.

The following should also be noted as covering the field of historical demography: *Population in History*, ed. D. V. Glass and D. E. C. Eversley, Arnold, London, 1965. Related to the foregoing works are the publications of the Milbank memorial Fund of New York, which deal with various subjects: *Current Research in Human Fertility*, 1955; *Trends and Differentials in Mortality*, 1956; *Thirty years of Research in Human Fertility*, 1958; *Population Trends in Eastern Europe, the USSR and Mainland China*, 1960; *Emerging Techniques in Population Research*, 1963.

A special study, of great interest, is that published by the Royal Commission on Population, under the following generic heading: *Papers of the Royal Commission on Population*, Vol. I. *Family Limitation and its Influence on Human Fertility During the Past Fifty Years;* Vol. II. *Reports and Selected Papers of the Statistics Committee;* Vol. III. *Report of the Economics Committee;* Vol. IV. *Reports of the Biological and Medical Committee;* Vol. V. *Memoranda presented to the Royal Commission;* Vol. VI. *The Trend and Pattern of Fertility in Britain*, London, Her Majesty's Stationery Office, 1949–54. Questions of great technical complexity are treated along with very easily understandable analysis. The whole is a model of a demographic balance sheet of a nation.

Most useful to the newcomer to the subject are works which summarize the progress of demography in accessible language, and which cover the whole field and principal findings. Simple treatments of particular subjects do exist: *Social and Economic Factors Affecting Mortality*, by B. Benjamin, Mouton, Paris, 1965; 'The Sociology of Human Fertility' by R. Freedman, in *Current Sociology* no 2. 1961.

Although a little dated and biased towards the United States, the following is probably the best general work: *Population*, by W. Petersen, The Macmillan Company, New York, 1961. The reader will find this book an excellent introduction, especially if he uses it in combination with the *Selected Readings*, which are very good anthologies of demographic literature and are not too technical: *Demographic Analysis*, Selected readings edited by Joseph J. Spengler and Dudley Otis Duncan, The Free Press, Glencoe, 1956; *Population Theory and Policy*, Selected Readings edited by Joseph J. Spengler and Dudley Otis Duncan, The Free Press, Glencoe, 1956; *Population and Society*, ed. Charles N. Nam, Houghton Mifflin Company, Boston, 1968; *Readings on Population*, ed. David M. Heer, Prentice-Hall Englewood Cliffs, New Jersey, 1968.

A more demanding technical introduction can be gained from *Techniques of Population Analysis*, by George W. Barclay, Wiley, New York, 1958; or from *Demographic Analysis*, by R. Pressat, Aldine Publishing Company, Chicago, 1970; or from the second edition of this work in French, *L'Analyse démographique*, Presses Universitaires de France, Paris, 1969.

Access to French materials opens up numerous new possibilities, notably *Cahiers de Travaux et Documents*, de L'Institut national d'études démographiques, Paris. These deal with various population questions (economy, active population, monographs on old parishes, under-development, geography of population, etc.) Also in French, the numerous works of Alfred Sauvy should be mentioned, especially: *Théorie générale de la population*, 2 volumes, Presses Universitaires de France, Paris; *Malthus et les deux Marx*, Denoël, Paris, 1963.

Finally, the periodicals totally or partly devoted to population can form a satisfactory introduction to the various aspects of the science of demography. The three principal ones are: *Population* (in French, notable for the variety of subjects dealt with); *Population Studies* (perhaps the most specialized of the demographic journals); *Population Index* (each number is composed of a short editorial, a comprehensive bibliography and important statistical tables).

For several years past, in the United States, *Demography* has collected the proceedings of the annual meetings of the Population Association of America. *Human Biology*, Wayne State University Press, Detroit, *Eugenics Quarterly*, American Eugenics Society, *Journal of Biosocial Science*, Blackwell Scientific Publications, Oxford, have wider interests and generally contain excellent studies on the area where demography merges into other disciplines (eugenics, biometry, and so on).

INDEX

abortion, 87, 88; in Japan, 120–1

age, 18, 120

ageing, 24, 25, 28, 29; among women, 30; consequences of, 30; differential, 26; effects on fertility, 32; effects on production, 32; effects on living standards, 32; in developed countries, 31; in electorate, 30; in France, 26; in Ireland, 26–7; in Sweden, 26; and medical care, 34; of élites, 28

age structure, 24

alcoholism, 47

Anglican Church, position on contraception, 58–9

anti-natalist policy, 118

Augustus, Laws of, 1, 113

average length of life, 38, 127

Besant, Annie, 57

Bills of Mortality, 2

birth control (*see also* contraception and neo-Malthusianism), 55; and Anglican Church, 58; and Catholic Church, 58; and differential fertility, 69; history of, 57; in Protestant countries, 59; in U.S.A., 57; spread of, 70; status of, 61; United Nations declaration on, 121

birth control movement, 56, 61

birth rate, 17, 136, 138, 139, 141; in France, 16, 114; in 19th and 20th centuries, 15; in U.S.A., 97; in western Europe, 96–7

Black Death, the, 14

Bradlaugh, Charles, 57

broken marriages, 86

Buddhism and birth control, 120

Catholic Church and contraception, 58, 64

China, population of, 12, 13

closed population, 144

Code de la famille, 114

comparative mortality, 43

conception, frequency of, 69

condition of mortality, 131

Condorcet, 6, 59, 112; *Esquisse d'un Tableau Historique*, 5

Confucius, 1, 111

consanguineous marriage, 78, 102

contraception (*see also* birth control and neo-Malthusianism): and abortion, 62; and fertility, 95; and Anglican Church, 58; and Catholic Church, 58

contraceptive methods, 123; and Catholic Church, 64; criteria of choice, 65; history of, 57; in Jewish households, 65; in U.S.A., 63; new methods of, 63

crude birth rate, 136, 138, 139, 141

crude death rate, 136, 140, 141

crude marriage rate, 136, 137, 140

current life table, 130

death rate (*see also* mortality), 15, 17, 137, 140, 141; in old age, 43

demographic analysis, 126

demographic evolution, 10